LOVING THE WHOLE PACKAGE

SHED THE SHAME AND LIVE LIFE OUT LOUD

JUNIE MOON SCHREIBER

PUBLISHING

Loving the Whole Package: Shed the Shame and Live Life Out Loud
By Junie Moon Schreiber

Crescendo Publishing, LLC
300 Carlsbad Village Drive
Ste. 108A, #443
Carlsbad, California 92008-2999
GetPublished@CrescendoPublishing.com
1-877-575-8814

ISBN: 978-1-944177-75-1 (p)
ISBN: 978-1-944177-78-2 (e)

Printed in the United States of America
Cover design by Melody Hunter

10 9 8 7 6 5 4 3 2 1

A Message from the Author

Welcome to this journey of loving your whole self. If you *only* read the book, that's more than awesome. There's a ton of information here to help you on your healing path, and there are powerful exercises to experience.

As you read my stories, ask yourself how they are similar to yours. They can offer you great insights into your own challenges.

Throughout the book you will see links to what I'm calling the Junie's Transformation Toolbox. This is special bonus material I want to give you as you read the book. I want to offer you the gift of some instructional videos, handouts, audios, and even access to the private "Loving the Whole Package" Facebook Group where you can connect with me and get your questions answered. I want to enhance your transformational experience, so the toolbox is filled with lots of goodies.

I want to add more value and deepen your experience, so I encourage you to go to midlifeloveoutloud.com/toolbox right now and find my most helpful and popular programs and courses to achieve the results you are seeking!

People are loving this book!

"I shared my personal journey with Shadow Work® in my book, *Practically Shameless*, and I intended to follow it with a companion book containing exercises and tools that people could use on their own. Then life took a turn, I became a caregiver and never got back to the companion book. Now my friend Junie Moon has written *Loving the Whole Package*, and I am thrilled to see that she has done what I couldn't do. In this book she has not only told her own story, not only shared her deep fears and her vulnerability and her moments of transformation, she has created a potent collection of exercises and tools so that many more people can change their lives as she and I have done with Shadow Work®. Well done, Junie!"

Alyce Barry
Author of *Practically Shameless*

"*Loving the Whole Package* provides an intimate, inspiring roadmap to help you embrace the light and dark within and live in freedom and joy."

Robin Rose Bennett,
Author of *The Gift of Healing Herbs and Healing Magic*

"Rather than resist what is, Junie Moon skillfully weaves the shadow with the light in such a way that allows them to dance with beauty and ease. Both revealing and raw, this book is a must-read for those on a journey of self-evolution."

Michael Neeley,
Host of the acclaimed Consciously Speaking Podcast and Mentor to Visionary Solopreneurs

"*Loving the Whole Package* is an offering of accessible insight and practical exercises to bring to light the way the hidden dark side, the shadow, affects your life. It teaches how to embrace it to fully love yourself, with all your perfections and flaws."

George Pitagorsky,
Author of *Managing Expectations: A Mindful Approach*

Table of Contents

Dedication

To my sweet mother, who through thick and thin, continued to love and support me always. I love you, Mom!

Foreword

By Cliff Barry, Founder of Shadow Work® Seminars

As the founder of Shadow Work® Seminars and having trained hundreds of facilitators through my thirty-plus years of teaching, I'm thrilled to see how this work is getting out into the world and reaching more people. The Shadow Work® model is my life's work, and it's very close to my heart. So when I see facilitators like Junie Moon taking this work out into the world, I am very pleased.

I have had the privilege of being Junie's trainer through these many years, certifying her as a group facilitator and coach in 2009. I've been watching her growth as a leader since then, but more importantly I have had the privilege of witnessing her transformation as a human being on her healing journey.

She's thanked me numerous times through the years for creating Shadow Work and for the gifts she's received, but it was she who showed up and embraced its practices. It was she that created her healing. She dove in and drank it all up. It touches me deeply to have had this effect on her.

The beautiful thing about Junie's journey is she helps others on *their* healing journey. That makes me very proud. She's dedicated to giving to others what she received: a more conscious life. That's what it's all about, helping others rediscover the truth of who they are. She gets that the meaning of this life is to become more enlightened. She understands that to have real spiritual connection, one needs to shine a light on the inner shadows, clean them up, and put them to work for you. She walks her talk, and in this book she shares her story to beautifully teach the opportunities Shadow Work® offers.

By sharing her story with painful honesty, she invites you into her world, which of course, shines a light into your world as well.

As I read the book and saw how she intertwined her transformation and my work, I was delighted and deeply moved. Because of Junie's revealing shares, I believe many will be touched.

She's real. With her story coupled with the Shadow Work teachings, I believe you will get a lot out of this book. She shared how this work brought her back to her true self, giving her a freedom and joy she never knew was possible.

Trademark notice: The term "Shadow Work®" is registered by the U.S. Patent and Trademark Office to Shadow Work Licensing, LLC., and is used herein with permission from Shadow Work Licensing, LLC. Only certified Shadow Work® Facilitators and Coaches may advertise or conduct self-improvement classes or seminars using the name Shadow Work®.

WAKE UP SWEET SOUL...

I believe...
You were born to be seen
You were born to share your gifts
You were born, at this time, this moment, to live your life fully
To shine YOUR divine light like no other can

BUT something has happened...
Life shaped you
Society
Well-meaning parents
Your religion
Your childhood friends,
EVERYWHERE...
You were given messages
You were told to be careful
To hide your light
To be a certain way
You were led to believe if you didn't follow the rules you would be
Judged
Abandoned
Unloved
Abused
Less than
AND NOW
You believe the big fat lie that if you really spread your wings, and
express your uniqueness, you will get hurt

In your conscious mind
You may not believe this
But unconsciously
There are old stories
Old tapes playing in your head
And you believe them

And they affect you
They sabotage you
They limit you
And they're running your show!

In this book I offer to you
My heart
My knowledge
My journey
The deepest place of my soul

I offer you special tools
New and improved lenses
For your eyes to see what's possible
And what's true

I offer you a peek into my unfolding as a way to invite you into yours

I have learned that by embracing my truth
Who I really am
Spirit in human clothing
AND learning that there is nothing inherently bad about me
AND dancing with vulnerability
Dancing with the fear
Letting people in
Showing people my heart
Sharing my truth
Risking that I may fall short in some ways and expose my imperfections
THAT I AM FREE!
Free to live fully expressed
Free to make bold moves
Free to breathe deeply
Free to allow love to flow into my heart and out to others
Free to be ME!

I share with you what I see as the biggest secret to living a full life...
Loving yourself in the deepest way

May you find your heart's calling and risk being seen. There is only one YOU and you are here for a reason. Shine your light!

Junie Moon Schreiber

How to Get the Most Out of This Book

There are three parts to the book:

The first part introduces you to the nuts and bolts of the transformation tools. There are exercises and loads of information to get you started.

The second part is filled with my vulnerable stories. By sharing my journey, you can see how all these tools can actually make an enormous impact on your life.

The third part offers you next-action steps, which will keep you focused and strong as your healing journey unfolds.

Take your time. Do the exercises. Allow yourself the opportunity to experience aha moments. Keep an open mind, and above all, breathe as you uncover hidden truths about yourself.

If there is one thing I want you to get from this book it is the deep knowing that healing is possible; you can transform your life. I did, and I know you can too. I dare you to turn your life into the greatest masterpiece it can be!

Introduction

Who Am I to Write This Book?

"Our deepest fear is not that we are inadequate. Our deepest fear is that we are powerful beyond measure."
– Marianne Williamson

Before we dive into the shadow realms and I share my story of transformation, I want to take a moment to tell you why I chose to write this book and how the creation of it was a journey itself.

Through the years, I had thought many times about writing about my transformative experiences, but frankly, my inner critic made me question whether I had the chops. I feared there were others more qualified than me, and the old "I'm not good enough" gremlin snatched my confidence, so I held back.

Who was I to step out?

Even as I approached the finish line and was getting ready to send the manuscript to the publisher, I experienced very uncomfortable moments.

I was scared.

Self-doubt reared its ugly head and had me in tears. This process was challenging. I had never done anything like this before, and I found myself in the "I don't know how to make this work" kind of place.

When I felt the fear, I allowed myself to drop into my vulnerability. I took a deep breath, held my heart, and let the tears flow. (I've learned that when I ignore my feelings, more pain is created.) I asked myself what was happening. Why was I feeling so vulnerable?

I was scared that it wouldn't be good enough! I was afraid I wasn't good enough! It's always the same friggin' thing! My "not good enough monster" snuck out and was jabbing my self-confidence.

This attack on my self-confidence made the process of writing feel daunting. There was a big learning curve to this whole booking-writing adventure, and it felt like a humongous mountain to climb. Even if I got to the top, would there be rainbows or thunderclouds waiting for me?

Hello, I'm Junie, a Recovering Perfectionist

Part of me was overworking to get this done and have it be brilliant. If it was great, then I wouldn't run the risk of being judged harshly. The very thing I had been working through the years to heal was in my face—my fear of falling short! So my perfectionist self showed up and tried to keep me from falling flat on my face.

Could I let myself be seen in my light? Could I risk being seen as just OK? After years of being told I was too bright and bubbly, after being hurt by others who judged my Junie-ness, could I actually let you into the most vulnerable places of my life?

I knew I could, and that I would, because something big happened to me last year and not doing it wasn't a choice.

It started back in August 2015 when Andy Golub, an internationally known body painter, agreed to appear on my TV program Life Out Loud with Junie Moon. As with all my guests, we jumped on the phone to discuss the upcoming show.

It was a great conversation. We had similar views about the body and our culture's demonization about it. We both see the body as a beautiful piece of work that shouldn't be hidden. It should be celebrated.

Then came the moment that blew me away: I asked him, "Would you paint me on the show?" and he said yes. My head spun a bit. Did I tell you he paints naked people?

I did something I never thought I could or would ever do: I took it all off and got painted. How could this be? I was the girl who almost threw up when I received invitations that included bathing suits and pools. I was the girl that was terrified to undress in front of boyfriends because I felt so ashamed of my body.

I couldn't believe I had come so far! I was finally comfortable in my own skin! It amazed me that after years of having intense self-hatred, I could do this!

A miracle had occurred. I'm not talking about the Red Sea parting or anything like that, but a shift in my perception. I saw myself through new eyes, through the eyes of love and acceptance. Something had truly changed, and I was compelled to share my story of transformation.

I knew in every cell of my being this message must be told because I knew I wasn't alone in the horrible self-hatred dance we do as women in this culture. I hired a videographer and created a mini-documentary called Shed the Shame, which I released in 2016.

I have to admit, I had some pretty big fear about releasing the film. I knew there was a huge chance someone would say something mean-spirited about my body.

- The naked truth: I'm fifty-three, and my boobs ain't what they used to be.

- The naked truth: I have meaty thighs that wiggle and giggle.

- The naked truth: I have stretch marks and bumps that do not allow me to fit the bill of what our society considers beautiful.

- The naked truth: I am perfectly imperfect, exquisite, and I love myself.

The great news is that over 15,000 people have seen the film, and only ONE person remarked that I should keep my clothes on. Not so bad!

Wanna see it?

Warning: There's nudity, cool music, tears, laughter, truth, and a whole lot of vulnerability. Here's the link to see it in Junie's Transformation Toolbox. midlifeloveoutloud.com/toolbox

I wanted to share my journey through this documentary in hopes of helping others know they are not alone in feeling hopeless and inadequate and that healing was indeed possible. I also wanted to share the tools I learned through Shadow Work® Seminars, tools that helped me heal a lot of my shame.

The response was beyond anything I could have anticipated. Many reached out to me sharing similar stories of self-loathing. People came to me in tears with thanks for telling my story, which really is their story. People said they felt more love of themselves and were grateful for the experience.

They also wanted to know how the heck I got to this place of grace and acceptance after years of intense self-hatred.

This book suddenly became a "must do." I had to write it and needed to share the struggles, the fear of not being enough, and what I discovered that led me to deep self-love.

This book is not about healing body shame and how I learned to love myself. It's about profound healing and loving the whole package, which freed my soul.

Do you want to have more joy in your life? Do you want more loving, intimate relationships and fulfillment? This book is about healing the core, wounding messages you picked up along the way that made you question your value as a human being. Once you learn how to retrain your thoughts, the world is your oyster, and life will never be the same again.

I wish you much healing.

Junie Moon

PS: If you haven't clicked the Junie's Transformation Toolbox link yet, do it now. I look forward to connecting with you there! midlifeloveoutloud.com/toolbox

Part One

*"You must go into the dark in order
to bring forth your light."*
– Debbie Ford

- 1-

In the Beginning...

*"One does not become enlightened by imagining figures
of light, but by making the darkness conscious."*
– C.G. Jung

When you were born, you were born with a full spectrum of personality. There were no limits. Anything was possible for you. You didn't censor yourself in any way. You were free to be you.

Think about it. When you were a baby, you cried if your diaper was wet or you were hungry. You laughed if something was funny. You didn't stop yourself from expressing your feelings. You were in the moment, and there was nothing telling you how to act, how to be, what to do or not to do. You just were.

You know how kids say the funniest things when you least expect it? That's because they just say what's on their minds. They're not thinking, "Should I say this? Should I act like that? What will they think?" They're not afraid of the judgment of others ... yet.

Shiny and New

I had no fear as a young kid. I was the happy-go-lucky child skipping through the fields. I had a bright, bubbly disposition and a bounce in my step. This was the true me, fully expressed, until I began learning that being bubbly had a cost.

I remember prancing around the garden apartment complex as a young child, accumulating smiles from the older folks that sat on their porches. It was great. I would smile and say hi, and they would light up. My light touched theirs.

All was divine in the world of Junie Moon until I began accumulating data that said being like this was bad. I learned there was a cost to appearing free-spirited, sweet, and bubbly.

As we all know, kids don't admire the teacher's pet! I was nine when the bullying began. Kids mocked me and pushed me up against walls, and I felt like something was wrong with me.

When I experienced this reaction to my light, I felt the pain of not being accepted. This took me away from the joyous present moment, and I got scared of expressing my inner light. Being me hurt.

The Data that Forms Your Life Blueprint

What a trip. One second you're a disembodied soul floating around, happy as a clam in some quantum-level soup, and the next, you're catapulted into an earthly body. To make matters worse, you weren't given any real guidelines on how to survive!

You were a blank slate of knowledge. You weren't given a How to Live on Planet Earth for Dummies manual. You were given squat. What a setup for disaster! You are suddenly in an earth suit trying to figure out how to live.

From your first breath, you began to pick up on the rules of life. You were told by your well-meaning parents (who didn't get any great manuals either) when to speak and when not to, how to be respectable, and what was a "no-no." You began to get punished if you spoke against them or if you didn't clean your room to a certain standard. You were being life schooled.

It wasn't just your parents either. Your culture and religion gave you their no-no's as well. At a young age, you took in a lot of information, and this created your own personal "how to live" rule book. Your experiences shaped your perception of life and the meaning you gave to everything.

The Programming

> *"Character is like a tree and reputation like a shadow. The shadow is what we think of it; the tree is the real thing."*
> – Abraham Lincoln

Not all the rules are handed to you in a safe, informative way; some you just experience. You might feel emotional pain associated with some life lessons, which strongly wires you as to what you can do and what you need to never do again.

This is the subconscious programming. If you felt shamed, judged, attacked, or hurt in any way, you figured out quickly how to never risk experiencing that again.

When you began to feel emotional pain or witnessed people experiencing pain at the hands of others (because of others' behaviors), you came to some very big conclusions. In fact, when you noticed "bad behaviors" in others that inflicted pain, you made decisions to never be like "that."

An example: Maybe when you were young, one of your parents yelled at you and frightened you. When your parent expressed anger, you might have felt unloved. As a kid, that's really scary. You're vulnerable and need your parent's love and protection.

There is a good chance that when you felt that fear, you decided that anger is dangerous and it hurts. You might have decided never to display that emotion to anyone because you wouldn't want someone else to feel unloved.

Another example might be that you witnessed one parent—let's say Dad—expressing rage to Mom, and you saw her cry. You might have thought, "That's horrible. My mom is suffering, and I would never want to do that to anyone."

It makes sense, right? Why would you ever want to act in a way that makes someone you love cry? The thing is, by saying you would never act like that (in this case, express anger), something very damaging happened. You threw the baby out with the bathwater.

That happens with every aspect of your personality that you decide is bad or shameful. If you decide something inside you is unacceptable and you try to push it down or away, you lose access to the gold in that part as well—you lose access to the baby.

In Shadow Work we say this is you disowning an aspect of yourself and putting it into a shadow. As stated from shadowwork.com: "The term 'shadow' was first used by Carl G. Jung to describe the repressed or denied part of the Self. Robert Bly popularized this idea in A Little Book on the Human Shadow. According to Bly, it was as if we threw these unacceptable qualities over our shoulder into a bag, which we've been dragging around behind us ever since." When you decide there is something you can't be like, you cut it off and fling it back in the shadow bag.

The problem is that you can't cut it off. It's a part of you—a valuable part of you. By denying its existence and tucking it away, you run a great risk that it will pop out when you least expect it. You can't seal the shadow bag shut and throw it away. It's energy, and it will find a way to be expressed. Sadly, if not harnessed and used consciously, it will leak out from the shadow bag as shadow and do the very thing you don't want—cause pain.

Beware of the Full Moon

Think about werewolf stories for a moment. The wolf was fine until the full moon came. She knew then it was time to lock herself up or people would die. People would be torn to pieces, with blood and ripped-up limbs everywhere. I know ... graphic. But seriously, that's what happens when we don't address the shadow that lives in the deep, dark cave of our psyche.

We lock away our demons, or parts that we think are bad, that we shouldn't expose to others. We hide them so deep in our consciousness that even we forget they're there until the full moon, until some event happens that accidentally unlocks the bolted dungeon of the unconscious mind and the monster appears.

We don't even see it coming. Maybe we've had a hard day or we're exhausted or we lose our job or our kid comes home with an attitude or ... something happens and it's the last straw and boom. ROAR!

We do our best not to be angry, or lazy, or mean, or arrogant, or act in some way that could be judged as negative or harmful, but it doesn't work. We can't stop being us. These parts are pieces of our whole. As I said, these parts are our essence and will be expressed.

We think we can just cut these parts off and never see them again, but the shadow monster is sitting off in the corner watching and waiting for the perfect moment to rear its ugly head. We must express all our self in some way. It hurts us to deny our true selves.

It's life force. The part has meaning, and we decided the meaning was bad. What if we could change the meaning and see it as good or maybe just as energy? What if we were able to use it for good?

The Hunt

We have to hunt the shadow, but a lot of the time we can't see it because we've pushed it so deeply into the corner it's invisible to us.

We need to track it by looking for the havoc in our life, for what's not working. What are the behaviors that are creating pain? Looking at what a person is actually doing that's making their life challenging can offer clues to the shadow.

In Shadow Work, we believe we must identify the "monster" and actually play with it. We need to find what is lurking in the shadows and invite it back into the light. We need to see it for what it is and consciously take back the power of this vital energy. We don't see it as a monster as much as an opportunity to embrace a vital piece of our being.

Once you learn how to tame it, it's no longer a scary monster. We can train these parts so that they are not demonic and harmful, but assets to our life instead. We must open the cage, release the shadow in a way that will not create any real-life consequences, and transform it.

If we don't, I can guarantee you that monster will find a way to come out. Either it will sneak out and hurt the very people you don't want to hurt, or it will hurt you.

"Everything that irritates us about others can
lead us to understanding ourselves"
– Carl Jung

Exercise:
Find out what's in shadow for you

Get a piece of paper and start to make a list of all the people you know that you don't like. Yep, think about the people that get under your skin. Take some time with this.

Next to each name, write the reason you don't like them. What is it about them that annoys you? What quality of their personality gets your goat?

Are they selfish? Self-absorbed? Greedy? Angry? Arrogant? Childish? Judgmental? Think about the qualities these people possess that you really dislike.

Now think about the people you really admire and list their names. What is it about them that you hold in high esteem? (You may find yourself thinking, "Oh I wish I was more like her!")

Are they go-getters? Creative? Funny? Successful? Playful? Sexy?

Now comes the fun part.

For both categories, dislike and admire, I invite you to consider whether you may have put this aspect of yourself in shadow.

You do your best not to exhibit the qualities you hate, right? Chances are you experienced those qualities as a young child and decided they were not good traits to have. You threw them in your shadow bag.

The same goes for the qualities you admire. Chances are you were shamed or you experienced those qualities as bad and threw them away too. We call them golden shadows.

You may have had really good reasons for disowning these personality aspects, but by throwing these parts away, you disconnected from your whole self.

Are you ready to reclaim your parts and feel the freedom of being fully you?

Might you want to reclaim the gold that lives inside your shadow?

Taking Your Power Back

Each part of you has great value. There is nothing inherently bad about you. It's all about how you use the energy. Each aspect has gold to be mined. In this work, we shine a light inside the bag and let those shadows out one at a time so that you get access to all of you in a controlled, empowering way. It's when we hide our parts and they disappear into the shadow realms that energy goes awry and people get hurt.

Remember, you can't suppress pieces of who you are. You are whole. You think you can slice away these parts and disown them, but you can't.

Here's another thing to think about: It takes a lot of energy to hold yourself back, to hold yourself down. You have to work very hard to keep these "bad" parts in the bag. When you embrace all your parts, you not only feel more powerful and energetic, you are free to be YOU fully!

Shining a light on the shadows and bringing them back to the forefront helps you consciously use the energies.

-2-

What Happened to Me?

*"We are shaped by our thoughts; we become
what we think. When the mind is pure, joy
follows like a shadow that never leaves."*
– Buddha

My parents were the best. They loved me with their whole hearts, and I was a very blessed child, … but I also picked up some messages along the way that had me terrified that I could lose their love.

I didn't know it at the time, but I was being programmed to fear loss. I picked up harmful strategies to keep me safe from risking loss, not knowing it would affect my future. It happened though, and I know it happened to you too.

If Looks Could Kill...

Did you have a parent who could, with that one look, make you feel like all the oxygen had gone out of the room? My mom had a look that killed. If I fell short in some way, I would see that look. My heart would jump into my throat, and I would feel unloved. That look said to me, "You screwed up! You should know better, young lady! You should know the rules and be the perfect little girl I'm always telling others you are."

Did she ever actually say these things? No. Was programming instilled in me about not messing up or I would be judged and lose love? Absolutely.

This was the setup: Mom was always complimenting me and pointing out to everyone how wonderful I was. She would say things like, "Look how put together June is. ... Look how responsible she is. ... Look what a bright spirit she is and how mature."

One would think that would be great for me, but I believed if I didn't act maturely, or if I wasn't the perfect child or broke one of her implied rules, I would drop off the pedestal as the golden child and I would be unlovable. This thinking created immense fear, which had me walking on eggshells.

It wasn't just my mom either. It was my dad too. I was the apple of his eye; the last thing I ever wanted to do was disappoint him, so I made damn sure I was the perfect little girl.

Because of my fear of losing love, I put my childlike, free-spirited part in my shadow bag and hired what we call in Shadow Work the Risk Manager. This internal part kept a watchful eye, making sure I didn't make any mistakes. I needed to be the responsible kid, so my Risk Manager created strategies that made me look like the perfect child, which kept me safe from being bad.

I was cherished, and that was a good thing. My Risk Manager made sure I didn't take any chances that would cause me to fall from grace, but there was a cost. Like I said before, there is gold to be mined in every aspect of who we are, and cutting off my childlike spirit limited my access to play and fun.

Holy Ground

Our parents are our gods, the people we put in the highest of high places. We want to please them. We want them to love us and take care of us. We will do whatever it takes to keep their love and stay connected, and that can cause us to lock away special parts of ourselves so that we don't risk losing their love.

I loved being the golden child; I felt superior to the other kids. While they were playing and being silly, I would converse with the adults. I felt special. While there's nothing bad about feeling special or even different, I paid a price. I was always assessing whether I was being as good as expected. I was deathly afraid of being bad.

I was scared that if my shiny casing cracked, my life would crash. My Risk Manager worked really hard, making me the perfect student and the best little girl possible. I would shine, shine, shine. It felt safe in the light, and everyone loved me—until they didn't.

Newsflash ...
Having a bubbly, bright, sunny disposition does not mean everyone will like you.

High Price to Pay

The overworking Risk Manager might have kept me from being reprimanded by my parents, but as an adult, there was a cost.

Because I was always so careful not to drop the ball, I became a control freak. My ex-husband (whom I will now lovingly refer to as my "wasband") called me the micromanaging queen, and he was right. I looked at everything a million times over.

I never risked making a mistake. I was constantly on edge and obsessing, which was exhausting. My Risk Manager was always on me to keep going, going, going and to look under every stone. I wouldn't allow myself time to just be. I couldn't relax.

I couldn't breathe until I was finally able to go inside that bag and reclaim my shadows. I was then able to trust the world wouldn't blow up if I didn't do everything.

When you learn how to access all of who you are, life changes!

-3-

Your Own Special Posse

"Great things in business are never done by one person. They're done by a team of people."
— Steve Jobs

Did you know you have your own powerhouse board of directors calling the shots in your life? Did you know this cast of characters offer different skills that create not only your inner emotional life but also the ability to influence your outside circumstances? Yep. Surprised me too.

You may have thought you're on your own with little influence over how your life turns out, but I'm here to share with you something profound: you have access to powerful parts inside you, special archetypal energies that I'm referring to as your board members that help you in ways beyond your wildest dreams.

I like to envision this panel of advisors as my best friends with superpowers. They are there for me at a moment's notice. They offer great advice, support, love, and action. They influence my every move, if I allow them in. Once you learn how to access these parts—their wisdom and their tools—life will never be the same.

Imagine you're the CEO of your life (which you are), and you have access to these parts that have great influence over the choices you make. If you don't listen to them, trust them, and welcome them into your day-to-day life, might you be missing out? Might you be stuck, or in pain, and not living a fulfilled life because you're flying solo and not using these great resources?

You can live your life without ever fully knowing your board, but let me just say that becoming aware of these parts and the roles they play and allowing them into your world is a total game changer.

Can you imagine feeling weak and stuck and then having access to a part that makes you feel powerful? If you struggle with overthinking, might it behoove you to access a part that can get you into action? If you're a dreamer and compulsive with your actions, might you want access—before you jump—to the part that is discerning? If you're sensitive and readily open your heart, might you want support and guidance so as not to risk getting overly vulnerable?

These are just a few examples of how things can go awry and how things can really work in your favor.

Your board works for you. Each member has the ability to use amazing tools to create a spectacular life. Isn't that great news? You have support! You have powerful, energetic parts ready and willing to serve you.

I had no clue that these highly skilled parts lived inside me. I was way out of whack with self-hatred and sabotaging behaviors that had tremendous consequences. Once I learned how to reel these parts in and align them with my highest wants, my life shifted in magical ways.

The 5 Musketeers

There are four archetypal energies that make up your kickass board, in addition to the Risk Manager I already told you about, the one who keeps an eye out for potential danger. The Risk Manager is a powerful gatekeeper, and one of its jobs is to guard the doorway to this panel. Each member has a purpose as well as superpower tools that influence you in creating a fulfilling life. When they're working together smoothly, you feel amazing.

As I mentioned before, the events in your life shape you, and these energetic parts get affected too—more like infected, actually. It's like your board member is sick. Until you offer it a transformational healing potion (for me it was Shadow Work) and get to your core issues, it can slack off with its job. One board member may not play nicely with another, causing quite the ruckus. One might be loud and overbearing while another feels like it has no place to be heard.

All the board members are important and honored. The intention is to get a nicely greased wheel, to get them to work hand in hand in your best interests.

-4-

Your Sovereign Self

"Being a star just means that you just find your own special place, and that you shine where you are. To me, that's what being a star means."
– Dolly Parton

The Sovereign board member loves you dearly and supports your passionate heart. She sees you for who you are, and she sees your gifts. When she's fully engaged, on board, and being heard, she tells you you're worthy and you believe her! You feel more than enough, and anything is possible. She's a good, yummy dose of pure, unconditional love.

Her power tool is blessing. She supports your vision. She touches your heart's desire and breathes life into your soul's mission. When you feel your Sovereign present, you feel whole and inspired, and you can shoot for the stars. When the Sovereign is strong, you feel deeply supported and seen.

Each board member has an emotion associated with it. When we feel the emotion, it's like a door opens and the part appears. For the Sovereign, it's joy. When we can access joy and let our hearts fill with passion, she appears.

A challenge can occur when the CEO (you) has received poor programming from some past experiences. If this happened, your Sovereign might have gone astray.

The messages received from the past can wound each archetypal energy and can knock them off their game. If the CEO got the message, "You're not good enough," the Sovereign will be affected (infected).

If you got this message that you weren't good enough (and frankly, I haven't met anyone who hasn't), your Sovereign can make you act in one of two ways. One is over-shining, where you try to prove your worthiness. The other way is you don't even try because you feel so unimportant you think, "Why bother?"

The Bright and Over-Shiny Star

> *"There is strong shadow where there is much light."*
> – Johann Wolfgang von Goethe

People that have an inflated, shining Sovereign can be seen as know-it-alls and full of themselves. They overshoot to show they are indeed worthy of love and accolades.

Aren't I Special?

I was the "look at me" girl. I went overboard and had people thinking I was too much. I was told I was too bright and to tone it down—literally. Ouch. I was so scared to look stupid that I overshot, and I tried so hard to be perfect, which then made me look quite arrogant.

On the outside, I looked like I had my act together. Underneath, I felt quite inadequate. I was terrified I didn't matter. I was terrified something was wrong with me. I felt like I wasn't good enough for anything.

I worked hard to show I was worthy of love, attention, and praise. I was the overachieving student, the people-pleaser, the anything girl to be as perfect as I could be. Anything less than perfect triggered my fear that I was not OK and put me at risk for not being loved.

By being larger than life, I appeared ungrounded and inauthentic. I was trying too hard to be liked, and it repelled people. There I was, trying to connect by being big and amazing, and the exact opposite happened. I didn't understand why I was so alone, why I was suffering, until I began healing my wounded Sovereign.

Why Bother?

In the opposite direction from the over-shiny Sovereign is the deflated Sovereign Self. When there is this wounding, this person feels so unimportant they think, "Why bother trying?" Everything feels hard, and it's like they have no spark left. Their star is hardly shining.

I've seen this pattern with clients. The wounding has made them go in the opposite direction. Instead of trying to prove they are good enough, they don't even try. It's like their dreams seem so farfetched that it's painful to think of what's possible. The thought, "Who am I to do something like ____," is common, so they stop dreaming or they dream but they never feel good enough to take that first step.

I know this deflated Sovereign syndrome too. I wasn't always just inflated. There were times when I felt I wasn't getting anywhere. I had been pushing myself so hard to get somewhere, to be loved, to achieve, only to burn out and crash. I began to feel like my aspirations were too hard, which confirmed I wasn't enough to make anything happen. My vision of what I thought was possible blurred.

The Healing: From Human-Doing to Human-Being

Both over-shining and failing to even try have costs. Both can make you feel spiritually vacant and alone. Inflation takes up a lot of energy and can push people away. Deflation keeps you from dreaming or going for your dreams because it seems completely out of reach. Both types of wounding in the Sovereign Self rob you of feeling fulfilled and living from a place of worthiness at the core.

Once I began healing my wounded Sovereign, I felt more grounded, connected to Spirit, and more authentic. I had a lot more energy because I didn't have to try so hard. I knew that inside I was a precious soul worthy of abundance and lots of love.

My clients, too, have found themselves with more energy and passion for life. They feel more whole and able to breathe.

Healing the Sovereign wound frees us. It allows us to deeply honor our unique light and embrace our divine gifts. Coming from a place of worthiness allows us to go for our dreams without burnout. We feel blessed as it allows us deeper connections with loved ones and we are able to shine our light, blessing the world.

Would you like to meet your Sovereign Self? Go to Junie's Transformation Toolbox and I'll take you on a meditative journey to connect with her.
midlifeloveoutloud.com/toolbox

-5-

Your Magician Self

*"A shift in perspective makes the particles in
your universe dance to new possibilities"*
– Anne Kagan

Can you believe you have your own personal Magician, guiding you with very wise eyes? This member of your posse looks out for danger and is the queen of discernment.

The Magician's power tool is detachment. She helps you step back, and she gives you perspective because when you're caught in the drama of life situations, your vision can get mottled. She helps you see better.

With her detached eye, she's able to look at your life objectively, without getting caught up in emotion, which is a very important skill. She assesses the outside situations and offers you options.

Even though the Magician can be detached from emotion, it has an emotion associated with it ... fear. Fear opens the door for the Magician to appear, and when you allow yourself to feel fear and not push it away, you can access the Magician's power tool, detachment. Then, you have the ability to step back and decide what needs to be done to keep you safe.

The wounding message that could infect your Magician Self is "You're bad." If you got that message as a young child, chances are your Magician is trying very hard to keep you from appearing bad.

Too Much Thinking

Just like your Sovereign Self, the Magician can be inflated or deflated. If a wounding inflates the Magician, you will feel overwhelmed. You may have a difficult time making decisions because the options your Magician gives you are endless.

People with inflated Magicians tend to appear as "in their heads" kind of people that don't seem to feel. Actually, though, they're feeling a lot … a lot of fear. They're afraid they might mess up and be seen as bad in some way. Because the fear is so great, the Magician will make the CEO—you—step back because she is deeply concerned. This type of wounded Magician will have the CEO overflowing with ideas and trying to figure out everything so that she can be in control, which leads to analysis paralysis.

Have you ever had a situation over which you just couldn't stop obsessing about what might happen? Maybe you couldn't sleep because your mind wouldn't shut up? Maybe you had to turn over every stone? When you feel out of control and overwhelmed, that's your Magician overshooting.

Once you learn how to invite your fear in and allow your Magician to support you in a healthy way, in balance with the other board members, you can assess your situation and act with much more success. Having a great idea that just stays in your head will not create a good outcome. (But you already know this, right?)

If you're a business owner, this is huge! Harboring too much fear of messing up will paralyze you. You might have a million awesome ideas, but you're not able to implement even one because you're terrified you might screw up. That's when you have to look to the other board members for support to restore your balance and make your business thrive.

I Can't See a Thing!

The opposite of the inflated Magician is the deflated Magician. This one can't see options at all and can appear dense, as though they have no ideas. Because of the fear of being seen as bad or of accidently acting badly, there is great risk attached to trying to figure things out. A person with a deflation like this will say things like, "I just don't know. I can't see a solution. There are no options."

Fear Not?

I want you to know that fear is your friend. It allows you to step back and make good choices. Your Magician board member is priceless, but if it's working time and a half, whether limiting your sight or flooding you with ideas, you may never move forward and embrace your God-given gifts. You're just too scared of being seen as a screwup.

You're here on this planet to live big and boldly. An unhealthy Magician keeps you from seeing clearly. If you can't see clearly, your decision-making skills will be impaired, and you'll find yourself making some pretty poor choices.

When you get your entire board to work together, your Magician will think more clearly and help you see what your options are that can bring you success.

Would you like to meet your Magician Self?
Join me in Junie's Transformation Toolbox
and I will take you on a meditative journey
to connect with her.
midlifeloveoutloud.com/toolbox

-6-

Right-Hand Woman to the Magician – The Risk Manager

"What happens if I try to build a life dedicated to avoiding all danger and all unnecessary risk?"
– Sam Keen

It's time to dive deeper into what the Risk Manager does. This powerhouse works with the Magician and plays an enormous part. I will be speaking a lot about its role throughout this book.

If your Magician sees you're unsafe, what's it going to do to keep you from getting hurt? It's going to do everything it can to keep you safe, so it calls in the Risk Manager. (You might say the Risk Manager is the hypersensitive assistant to the Magician.) After consulting with the Magician and learning the CEO's history, the Risk Manager's job is to assess the situation even further and then whip up strategies to stop the CEO from taking any unwarranted chances. She often appears as negative self-talk, certainly stopping you from moving forward.

She can tell you things like:
You can't do that.
Who do you think you are?
You're not smart enough!
You're not pretty enough!
You're past your prime!
You're not good enough!

These critical thoughts are a great strategy to keep you from taking risks, but your Risk Manager can also use bodily sensations like nausea, headaches, and confusion to stop you from taking risks. If your Risk Manager is scared you'll drop the ball or get hurt in some way, it will be on high alert. Her job is to slow you down and keep you out of harm's way.

As I mentioned previously, when I was being bullied as a kid, there was great risk in being seen. If I raised my hand in class and answered a question correctly or incorrectly, some horrible comment was bound to follow and cut me to the core.

My Risk Manager would tell me things like: "You aren't that smart. You don't know the answer, so don't even try." That was a great strategy to keep my light dimmed and my mouth shut.

She also gave me chest pains to distract me. Instead of participating in school, I was in the nurse's office, begging to go home. My Risk Manager worked constantly to hide me in the background. Keeping a low profile decreased my risk of being ridiculed by the other kids.

I call her the gatekeeper to deeper healing. She's looking out for you all the time to see if you're safe. If she thinks you are at high risk, she won't let you speak to the other members of the board. After all, if you can't work with the other players, you don't have access to their superpowers, which keeps you out of balance and severely limits your healing journey. You must get your Risk Manager on board; once you do, the sky's the limit.

Ooh Baby, Don't Stop!

Sorry, but we as human beings are wired for survival, not for pleasure. If you are in bed having the best sex ever and your house is burning down, you ain't gonna stay horizontal. You will flee the burning house and pick up later where you left off.

That's what the Risk Manager does—she watches out for danger. She knows how you've been hurt in the past and is on guard to sniff out any risks that might appear again. She's been with you since you began learning life's do's and don'ts. She's looking out for you.

Frankly, she doesn't even care if you're happy. She wants to make sure you're not at risk for pain. She has a job, and she's going to take it to the max unless she sees the strategies she's been using aren't working.

As we get older, we may need to give the Risk Manager an update. She's been around since you were so small that she might think you're still five and may still be overly protective. She may be overworking and causing havoc in your life without knowing it.

Working with your Risk Manager can create great opportunities for sustainable transformation. When you build a relationship with her and show her how some of her strategies are not working, she will give you room to make some different choices in your life. Befriend her!

Hey, Why Didn't This Work?

Have you ever gone to a transformational weekend only to slip back into sabotaging behaviors a few weeks later? It's your Risk Manager's job to keep you from taking big risks, so when you suddenly experience a big change, her ears perk up.

Change is extremely risky business. Your Risk Manager is constantly thinking, "What might happen if _____ happens?" You need to get her on your side and make her see that the change you're embracing is a good thing, and she will keep you from pain. She needs to see the old strategies are actually causing more harm than good. Once she sees that the cost of not changing is more painful to its CEO, she will look for more solutions to keep you out of pain.

Most personal-growth and spiritual programs bypass your fear and push you into the manifestation stage without looking at the risks. I think most people are afraid of fear and think if they go there, there won't be healing. The exact opposite is true. By allowing the fear in and working with it, you can then open yourself up to all the possibilities.

Many of these other programs focus on positive thinking and work on your mind-set of "anything is possible." Yes, anything is possible, but if you don't flush out your subconscious concerns—look out. Your Risk Manager will go into high gear to keep you from stepping out of your comfort zone and do what it takes to slow you down.

Looking under the covers can feel scary. You may want to run the other way rather than see what monster might be hiding under there. If you don't peek, you will never truly get your Risk Manager on your side. Once this powerhouse part assesses what's really risky and what's just old, useless programing, you can move forward and the transformation will hold. Good news, huh?

Would you like to meet your Risk Manager? Join me in Junie's Transformation Toolbox and I will take you on a meditative journey to connect with her. midlifeloveoutloud.com/toolbox

-7-

Your Warrior Self

"Anger is just anger. It isn't good. It isn't bad. It just is. What you do with it is what matters."
— Jim Butcher

Imagine having a sword at your side, ready to slice if necessary to keep you alive. How cool is it that you have a Warrior Self willing to step up for you? Her job is to set healthy boundaries so that you know where you stand. She helps you say "yes" when you mean "yes," and she helps you say "no" when you really need to set a limit and say "no."

She also gets you moving. You can have the greatest ideas and passion in the world, but if you don't have your Warrior team player alongside you, moving you along, you ain't going nowhere! When you feel safe and have a clear vision from your Magician, and when your heart is pumped up by your Sovereign, your Warrior knows how to get things done!

This board member's superpower is the ability to draw that proverbial line in the sand so that you know who you are separate from others, and she gets you rocking in your life.

The emotion that opens the door to this energy is anger. When we can access our anger, when we allow it in and don't push it away, this powerful energy can set healthy limits. Feeling the "ouch" allows the Warrior to step in and communicate effectively what is not acceptable in the CEO's world.

Anger gets a bad rap in our culture, collectively shaming people who express their anger. Yes, anger can hurt people when used out of shadow, but if we learn to access it consciously in a grounded, effective way—the way most of us have not been taught—an inner strength shows up and shift happens.

You want to see an end to world hunger? You want to see governments act with integrity and transparency? You want to see change in the world that saves our oceans and keeps our earth alive? When people really access their anger and allow their Warrior to show up, treaties are signed, speeches are heard, and worldwide transformation can occur.

Just like the other members of the posse, this member can become inflated or deflated due to past programming. The wounding message that infects the Warrior Self is "You do not exist" or "You do not exist separate from others."

The Warrior Self's job is to protect the CEO's identity at all cost.

> *"Whatever we refuse to recognize about ourselves*
> *has a way of rearing its head and making*
> *itself known when we least expect it."*
> — Debbie Ford

The Bully

The Warrior wants the CEO to feel it has the power, so she will work hard to let others know who's boss. If she has the wounding that she doesn't exist, she's going to be in people's faces and let them know who's in charge. She needs to push up against another's boundary to feel her existence.

This type of overshooting can rub people the wrong way, scare people, or hurt people because it's bully energy. She can be loud, obnoxious, rude ... anything to get her point across that the CEO is better than the opponent.

The Doormat

The deflated Warrior can appear to have no power at all and tends to acquiesce, in the name of survival, when confronted. If someone crossed the CEO's boundaries when she was young, she may not know how to handle conflict in a healthy way. Sadly, this is something I know very well. Remember the bullying?

There was one kid in particular ... I called her my nemesis, and she got in my face often. If I pushed back, it got worse. I learned if I kept my mouth shut and blended into the background the best I could, the bullying was minimal.

She overpowered me. There was no real line in the sand that kept her and her pack at bay. My personal space was violated on a regular basis, and not just physically either. I was taunted in front of the other kids, which regularly made me feel powerless, inferior, and extremely threatened.

Having been trained as a young girl in the skills of retreat and hide, my Warrior learned how to keep me safe by keeping me quiet. This had a major effect on my marriage (more on relationships in chapter thirteen). Let me just say that playing it small and hiding your truth has a big cost.

Having the Sword at Your Side

Suffice it to say that having a healthy Warrior keeps you from harm. When this board member is functioning, you can speak your truth, set your boundaries, and take action. This part helps the CEO create amazing relationships and successful careers and to feel powerful inside.

> Would you like to meet your Warrior Self? Join me in Junie's Transformation Toolbox and I will take you on a beautiful meditative journey to connect with her.
> midlifeloveoutloud.com/toolbox

-8-

Your Lover Self

*"The ocean stirs the heart, inspires the imagination
and brings eternal joy to the soul."*
– Wyland

Lastly, you have your Lover on the board, the part that helps you receive love and give love to others and yourself. The Lover helps with the flow of energy between you and another. She helps you embrace your feelings, which further invites love in and builds deeper connections.

The emotion that opens the door for this board member to appear is grief. When we feel sadness, it opens our hearts and allows deeper connections to everything. Think about it: if you're hurting and post on Facebook you're in pain, what happens? A flooding of hearts appears on your timeline. Don't you feel a deeper connection to your friends? Don't you feel more loved? Your Lover part helps you get what you need so that you don't feel alone.

This is also where your sensuality and sexuality live. If this board member is functioning well, it allows the profound bonding of two people. She allows you to feel your vulnerability so that you can allow another into your life.

The Lover isn't a heady part like the Magician who can be detached from emotions. This part is the opposite; she lives in your body and gives you access to all your emotions. When you can go inside and experience bodily sensations, you feel more connected to everything. Yes, sadness brings out your Lover Self, but when you go within, your body talks to you, and you have full access to all your feelings.

For example, if you're in a precarious situation and feel your throat close up, you are most likely feeling fear. This allows you to call upon your Magician for help. Maybe you feel a painful emptiness in your solar plexus, so you go inside and realize someone is trespassing on your personal space. You call upon your Warrior to step up and protect your boundaries.

This board member gives you valuable information by allowing you to hear the body's messages, which then gets you the support you need. Your emotions are invaluable. The power tool used by this member is the body and the ability to know what it's saying. By connecting to your body, much wisdom is revealed.

In Shadow Work, we believe the Lover was the first to appear in your life. When you were born, you were dependent on others for survival. You can't be more vulnerable than that! You had needs that had to be met. Your Lover has the superpower to connect with others and get what you need.

This is also where your inner child lives. It's a place of wonder and sweetness. This is the untouched, innocent arena where, when it's functioning in a healthy way, it allows you to play and access your creativity. When we have wounding in this energy, we can put our childlike spirit in shadow.

As children, we had desires and looked out into the world to get our needs met. As you know, we didn't always get what we wanted and felt let down. We often idealized something we wanted, like a new toy, and then our Sovereign Self got motivated to make it happen. She wanted us to feel happy and fulfilled.

If our needs didn't get met, we felt betrayed. Part of growing up is learning how to handle the feelings of betrayal, and with a healthy Lover, you can.

Like the other members of the board, here too is a wounding message that, when you received it as a child, infected the Lover. The wounding message is "You are not loveable" or "You don't know how to love right."

Overflowing with Love

When the Lover is not up to par, she will go overboard trying to prove she's loveable or loving, making the CEO appear very needy. The overflowing Lover energy is desperate to get connection and wants the CEO to appear as loving, so she may be overly touchy/feely. She overshoots. She also might cry a lot in hopes of getting sympathy, a.k.a. love. Surely if we show we're really hurting, we'll get help, right? Unfortunately, that's not always the case.

This is the inflated version of the Lover. By being overtly loving or needy, the Lover member can overwhelm people. She's trying to connect, but she's too much for others.

Someone overflowing like this might appear to have an abundance of victim energy. When we witness this sort of behavior, one of two things might happen. We might run in the opposite direction because we think they will suck us dry, OR if we have an inflated Sovereign wounding, we might be drawn to this person and want to rescue them! Interesting, huh?

I Feel Nothing

In contrast, the deflated Lover appears more stoic. While the inflated is overflowing, the deflated version loses access to feeling. Due to experiencing betrayal at a young age, the Lover shuts down the feelings.

There was a time in my twenties when I couldn't cry. Not a tear. I knew I was sad, but I was so far from allowing myself to feel. Why? I had experienced the ultimate betrayal when I was fourteen: my dad died, and I felt abandoned. I will share more in later chapters about that experience and how it shaped my life, but for now, let me say I never felt more alone than when he left this planet. I never wanted to experience that grief again, so my Lover deflated and squashed my vulnerable self.

This action, this deflation, locked my sweet inner child away and made me grow up quickly. There was no place for needs and certainly no place for expressing my feelings. I learned at fourteen that love could be taken away in a heartbeat and leave me stranded. I felt the loss, then I felt unloved.

Love, Love, Love (Tune of the Beatles)

"You have been criticizing yourself for years, and it hasn't worked. Try approving of yourself and see what happens."
– Louise L. Hay

On my grandmother's deathbed, she said, "Love is the answer to everything." When she spoke those words, I was taken aback because she wasn't one to speak like this. I guess when one is letting go of one's life, walls melt and truth appears.

I always say that love is stronger than fear and can move mountains. It can feel scary to be vulnerable and show our underbelly, but when we heal and get this powerful part we call the Lover working properly, we open ourselves up for deeper connection to all those we come in contact with. When this profound healing occurs, we feel the connection to All That Is and our vulnerability is seen as a blessing.

My biggest wound has been losing my dad. I needed to work with all my board members to restore balance, but it was my Lover that needed the most attention—and she still does. I was hurt, but thankfully I realized that closing off my heart and hiding myself away were too high of a price to pay.

By closing off my heart, I missed out on true intimacy. I let people in just so far. I tended to look for problems in my relationships, and as you know, if you seek, ye shall find! If I sensed I could get hurt, I bolted.

> *"Courage starts with showing up and*
> *letting ourselves be seen."*
> – Brene Brown

I have experienced the most amazing things by exposing my true self and revealing my vulnerability. I want to scream from the rooftops that vulnerability is a superpower. When we hide any part of ourselves, we lose our potency and ability to feel alive.

Love, guys. Love and allow love in. There is nothing more powerful on the planet than love.

Would you like to meet your Lover Self?
Join me in Junie's Transformation Toolbox
and I will take you on a beautiful meditative
journey to connect with her.
midlifeloveoutloud.com/toolbox

-9-

When Everyone Works and Plays Together Nicely

"Teamwork makes the dream work."

In Shadow Work® we see these five board members as the foundation for both your survival and your ability to thrive in your life. We need them to work properly and together. They each play an important role, and when one of the energies is behaving badly—like an overbearing board member who thinks it's their way or the highway—there is imbalance. Some members might skirt their responsibilities or, worse, hide in the closet during important board meetings! Teamwork is a must for healthy living.

When these parts are healthy and strong, we thrive. When one of these parts has been injured, there will be discord. We must look to the past to see what happened to throw these energies off (the wounding) and restore them to balance if we are truly to live a fulfilled life.

Where to Start?

*"We find that by opening the door to the shadow
realm a little, and letting out various elements a few
at a time, relating to them, finding use for them,
negotiating, we can reduce being surprised by
shadow sneak attacks and unexpected explosions."*
– Clarissa Pinkola Estés

After learning about your council of wisdom, you might be wondering where the heck to start! There might be a board member you want to rein in because it's inflated. You might want to go directly to the little girl that needs help right now.

As shadow workers, we always start by asking the client what they want to have happen. Once we are clear what they want in their life and how they want to feel, we look for the "bad guy." What is it that is getting in their way? Where are the wounds?

Then we begin to bring out the different parts and interview them. We take a step back and put the parts "on the carpet" to explore. For example, we might want to look at the voice that says, "You're bad!" So we look at that part as if it was separate from us. (They do this in psychodrama.) By separating ourselves from this part, we can get our Magician to look at it objectively.

We often ask these parts, "How much airtime do you have in your CEO's head?" If one member is overworking, overreacting, or taking up a lot of space, another part is feeling unseen, unheard, and squashed. We need each part present, playing its role, and working together with the other parts so that there is harmony.

When we find the "out of control" board member, we don't fire it. We don't shame it. We don't even focus too much on its behavior. Pointing a finger at it and saying, "You're behaving badly!" can add insult to injury. That's how it got wounded to begin with, so the last thing we want to do is injure it more. That's why we look for the board member that is in the background, hoping to be seen and heard. We need to create space for this part so that healing can occur.

There is Hope!

When I first began to understand that I had this powerhouse board and learned that a wounding had caused them to act as they did, I thought I was really messed up! I saw my Magician being obsessive, which had my Risk Manager frantic. Both had me over thinking and watching for risks at every turn. I saw my Warrior was paralyzed which prevented me from speaking up and from setting healthy boundaries, and then she would make me rage out of control when pushed to the edge. I saw my wonderful Sovereign Self with great dreams, but due to the wounded part inside me that felt unworthy, it was stopped. And lastly, I saw a very sad Lover whose heart had been broken and who was extremely scared to connect. What a mess I was.

Here's the good news: healing is possible! You have taken a giant first step by reading this book, and coupled with the toolbox, you will begin a deeper transformational journey to free up your soul. My life is a testament that this powerful transformational path works. I also get to see it profoundly affect my clients' lives as well. So take a breath, keep an open mind (as best you can), and continue to dive into this shadow world.

Part Two

"And the day came when the risk to remain tight in a bud was more painful than the risk it took to blossom."
– Anaïs Nin

-10-

Risk Manager to the Rescue

*"We don't want to EAT hot fudge sundaes as much
as we want our lives to BE hot fudge sundaes.
We want to come home to ourselves."*
− Geneen Roth

For years, I was completely allergic to conflict. If someone I loved became angry, I felt like my heart was being ripped out of my chest and I couldn't breathe. I would panic. I wanted to run for the hills and escape.

Since the hills were inconvenient, I ran to food, which helped me escape the pain, distracted me from my feelings of inadequacy, and numbed me. Food was my friend, my go-to, my confidant. Food was my over-the-counter prescription that got me through the day.

Conflict felt like death to me; it was my enemy. I may not have broken out in hives or gone into anaphylactic shock, but it did indeed feel like I was suffocating.

It's really not even about the conflict but the anger—what anger meant to me, how anger felt. To me, anger meant I did something wrong in someone else's eyes and that I was bad and unlovable, which made me feel terribly alone. I hated anger, and I would do anything not to feel it or engage with it.

Conflict = Anger = Disconnection = Death

Food, on the other hand, made me feel loved and connected. It didn't fight back. It didn't tell me I was bad. It was accessible and reliable. It helped me connect to myself, and it felt like I was loving myself by treating myself to something sweet.

In addition to the sweetness, it was easy to get. I didn't have to go to the doctor and tell him the embarrassing symptoms I was experiencing from anger: the shame, the fear of being abandoned, and that I felt terribly alone.

I could get food at a moment's notice, and I didn't have to drive to a dark alley and find the local dealer to get my stash. I only had to walk to my fridge, and I'd be all set. No one would have to know.

If someone was around and I didn't want them to see me communing with Ben and Jerry (two of my closest friends way back when), I would drive to the local 7-Eleven and grab my jumbo Kit Kat bar.

I liked to eat when no one was looking, and eating in my car on the way home was awesome. I felt free ... powerful. I'd blast some Led Zeppelin and enjoy the high! I was alone with my lover and dear friend, FOOD, and I could enjoy it without anyone's judgment.

Car eating—that was my sneaky place where I could become invisible and do what I needed to do. It was the safest of places for me where no one would see me shooting up my sugar to get my fix, where I could disappear and not feel.

As great as food was when it came to helping me calm down, feel love, and avoid conflict, the strategy had dire consequences. It was a temporary solution with long-lasting side effects.

It led to massive weight gain, physical discomfort, and of course, self-loathing. I may have avoided the wrath of someone's anger, but inside, I had tremendous conflict and extreme anger toward myself. My Risk Manager worked hard to keep me from feeling unloved, but it didn't realize the consequences were happening anyway. The very thing it wanted me to avoid was still happening, just in a different way.

In 2002, I hit 200 pounds, and I felt horrible. I had gone up and down the scale forty to fifty pounds at a time in previous years, but this was different. I had lost a substantial amount of weight in 1999 and thought I licked the problem. I had started attending Overeaters Anonymous, a twelve-step program modeled after AA. Once I got to a small size and felt my relationship with food was healthy, I stopped attending meetings. I thought I had it under control.

I hadn't done the program as they suggested. I did certain recommended steps and left out what didn't resonate with me. I was a bit cocky since I was losing the weight and getting away with not doing the whole program. Once I lost all the weight, I bolted. When I found myself back up the scale (and worse than ever), I hit rock bottom. This time I was not only horribly overweight, I was also physically uncomfortable and in deep emotional pain.

I had only scratched the surface of my compulsive overeating back in 1999. Little by little, I began to use food as I had previously. It was my coping strategy, but it stopped working because of the nasty side effects.

My dark night of the soul with this issue occurred after my wasband and I purchased an RV. Our plans were to hit the road for a great adventure. I was excited but also scared of being on the road for so long with my son, who was very young. I was very conflicted and stressed to say the least.

We had bought the RV off eBay, and the guy who sold it to us stocked the fridge with a shitload of candy. Every day, whenever I could, I would sneak out to the RV and grab a mouthful. I remember feeling anxious at night while trying to get my son to sleep and being very short with him when he didn't go to bed fast enough. I couldn't get to the RV soon enough for my fix. The candy was calling my name and I felt intense anxiety. I tried to push my discomfort away, but I was out of control.

Then my emotions would spill out onto my son and wasband. It wasn't pretty.

I couldn't focus on anything other than getting back out to the RV. My mind was running amok, and I knew this was not normal. I needed help.

> *"It is in your moments of decision*
> *that your destiny is shaped."*
> – Tony Robbins

That's when I made the greatest decision. I decided to just eat whatever I wanted to eat and to enjoy the trip without hating myself. Then, when I came back, I would go back to Overeaters Anonymous and get the help I needed. I had not fully done the program, and they appeared to have the answer I was looking for. Plus, I was desperate. My old reliable friends Ben and Jerry were hurting more than helping.

Overeaters Anonymous was an amazing tool for me. It helped me "get clean" with food and to see how I used food as a drug to avoid my pain. I learned a lot about myself in Overeaters Anonymous, and it was a great first step to my healing.

Once I added Shadow Work® to the mix, life changed dramatically. I finally understood why I used food as my drug. I was able to shift the old, fearful wiring that led to the overeating to a healthier dynamic.

I lost a significant amount of weight and have been in the same size body for fourteen years! Anyone who has struggled with the up-and-down drama of weight gain knows the challenge of keeping the weight off. I could say this was a miracle, and it certainly feels like grace, but really, it was about finally getting to the deep, unhealthy roots that infected my soul.

The Quick Fix Drug and Its Dire Consequences

SURGEON GENERAL'S WARNING:

Unhealthy eating will give you a sense that all is well. It will ease your troubles, calm your nerves, give you a feeling of power, and make you feel loved, safe, and happy. Some people actually feel euphoric and get a burst of energy, enabling them to do whatever they think they can't do typically in their life.

Side effects include:
Weight gain
Feelings of inadequacy and unworthiness
Self-hatred
Sadness
Loneliness
Physical pain due to extra stress on the joints
Loss of money due to constant revamping of one's wardrobe

Consult your personal-growth provider immediately if you experience these symptoms on a regular basis.

-11-

Why Did My Risk Manager Pick Up This Costly Strategy?

"Love yourself first and everything else falls into line. You really have to love yourself to get anything done in this world."
— Lucille Ball

I think at the root, we all want and need love, period. When we feel love, it connects us to The Source, to Spirit. It helps us relax and know we are not alone.

Love can come in many shapes and sizes, and we need love to survive. We need that connection to others. I had the great blessing to experience love deeply as a child as I was extremely close to my dad. He was my everything, and as I mentioned earlier, at the young age of fourteen, I lost him, the most important person in my life, which brought me the horrible pain of losing connection to someone I loved deeply.

It was June of 1978 when he got really sick and was diagnosed with brain cancer. By mid-June, he had surgery to remove the cancer. He underwent radiation to get rid of the rest, and the prognosis (as I remember) was hopeful. We bought some time.

He seemed to be holding on and even getting some strength back, but in September of 1978, he had a brain bleed and was gone.

I tell you this because this experience shaped my life on so many levels. To this day, I continue to unfold the layers of the impact of this tragic summer.

As I continually say, our experiences shape us, and those three months that led to my dad's death gave me a bunch of messages that have affected me profoundly. This loss laid down a load of programming, and I continue to this day to cut the wiring and heal.

The Wiring

I relied on my dad in so many ways. Firstly, he was my loving father, always there with a hug for me after a long day of bullying at school. I would cry in his arms, and he would comfort me.

He also was my cheerleader and buddy. He helped me with my homework and with memorizing my lines for the plays I performed in. I was the apple of his eye, and I felt adored. He was my rock, my king, my go-to for support.

So what happened to me when my dad was ripped out of my life? I got the message that people I love—and who love me—leave me. I learned that I can't rely on anyone to be there or trust that they will stick around. I wasn't safe to love. On some level, I believed that if I opened my heart, I risked being abandoned.

There was great risk in loving someone. When bumps appeared in my relationships and disturbed the peace, I felt threatened, as if the wound was reopened and I was losing love again. My Risk Manager would sniff out anything that looked like conflict, and if it sensed adversity, it was time to get the heck out of Dodge as soon as possible.

Looking back at my relationships, I see how difficult it was to open up to anyone fully or rely on them. When my dad left me, I learned that nothing is guaranteed, and life can change in a heartbeat.

My dad's diagnosis was not only a death sentence, it also turned him into a monster. Yes, a monster. They cut out a piece of his brain, and it changed his personality. He looked like Frankenstein with a shaved head and ugly stitches that I had to see five days a week as I wheeled him down the hospital corridor to get his treatments.

My mom said I didn't have go with him for his treatments, but that wasn't an option. I wanted to do anything I could to keep him alive, to support his survival. In the end, it just wasn't enough to keep him here.

I remember one day in the waiting room, he began preparing me for his departure, saying things like, "You'll be OK if I'm not here, right?" I would have no such talk. As soon as he began speaking about dying—or, in my mind, giving up—I put a stop to it. That was way too painful to consider and I wouldn't hear of it.

Another thought I had when he seemed to be giving up was maybe I wasn't enough to keep him here! If only I could give more, be more, then maybe he would try harder to live. When he died, I had the thought that I hadn't been enough, a belief that still challenges me to this day with relationships. Am I enough?

> *"It's not the events of our lives that shape us, but*
> *our beliefs as to what those events mean."*
> – Tony Robbins

Ah, the beliefs we pick up!

The beliefs I acquired from losing my dad:
I'm alone.
I have to take care of myself.
Trust no one.
Maybe I'm not good enough to stick around for!

When I heard my dad was gone, I curled up into a ball on my sheepskin rug in my room, thinking, "How will I survive without him?" That was my Magician kicking in to figure out a survival plan. You see, it wasn't just that I lost my dad—I lost him during one of the hardest times in my life. The school kids were being nasty to me, I didn't feel close to my mom, and I felt very alone. My dad was my one and only go-to, so when he left this planet, I truly felt the world stop.

The fear made my Magician appear and helped me take a step back and look at my options. My mind was racing, and I was terrified. That's when it called in its assistant, the Risk manager, to create the strategies to keep me alive.

To this day, I can find myself overthinking my way through uncomfortable experiences. If conflict arises (which, as I said before, feels like death to me), my Risk Manager's ears perk up. It doesn't want me to feel anything like the loss of my dad ever again, so it steps in quickly. I don't get stuck there or feel the anxiety I used to, but it can still happen. The good thing is I catch it early, and I can shift it quickly.

There's nothing wrong with strategizing to avoid conflict, but the way that my Risk Manager had been managing my discomfort was the problem. It had me eating boxes of Oreos to feel love and hiding from true intimacy. Instead of allowing me to be vulnerable and feel what I needed to feel—or ask for help—my Risk Manager would have me check out and dive into sugar. My Risk Manager wanted me to gain back control as soon as possible and avoid the pain of conflict. It was one way to go, but there was a high price to pay.

How I Acquired the New Wiring

Once I began talking with my Risk Manager, things changed. I got her to see that numbing out with food made me miss out on true connection, which led to terrible feelings of loneliness. By anesthetizing myself with sugar, life was harder. Food made things worse, and the last thing my Risk Manager wanted was for me to feel worse.

Yes, there's risk in losing someone, but the cost of not connecting authentically is way more painful. I needed my Risk Manager to know things had changed. She needed to know I was an adult now and was willing to take the risk of loving and even losing. I wanted a healthy relationship. I wanted a healthy body and deeper connections.

She needed to know I'd grown up. I wasn't the extremely vulnerable fourteen-year-old anymore. I had supportive friends and transformational tools, so if I did bump into uncomfortable situations, I'd be able to handle it differently.

I'm grateful for my Risk Manager. She helped me through some very tough times when I didn't know how to handle my life. She helped me stay away from conflicts that I had no skills to handle and helped me remain invisible when the kids were crushing my spirit.

She saved me from terrible pain when I was a kid, but she needed to be reprogrammed! It was time to emerge into the twenty-first century. I needed to upload the new software.

My eating has been in check for a while now, and I have a healthier relationship with food. I don't use food as a drug anymore, and I enjoy it in a way I never could have in the past. I'm not perfect, and sometimes I find myself in the cookie jar, but I catch myself, take a breath, and look deeper into the reason I'm acting out. Instead of months or years of crazy eating behaviors, I can have an episode and then get back on track.

I don't want to just throw my Risk Manager under the bus. She wasn't the only one that had to get up to speed. My other board members needed to be addressed as well.

-12-

Not the Only Guilty Party

*"Real transformation requires real honesty. If you
want to move forward, get real with yourself."*
— Bryant McGill

I can't solely blame my Risk Manager for my sabotaging behaviors.
My other board members weren't cutting the mustard either. By
acting out of shadow, the other parts created dire consequences for
me. Yes, my Risk Manager's job was to do something—anything—
to keep me safe from experiencing inadequacy, shame, sadness,
fear, and anger, but there were also:

- My Warrior, who needed to set good boundaries and stand
  up for me

- My Sovereign, who needed to support me and let me know
  I'm worthy

- My Magician, whose job was to help me step back and look
  objectively at my options

- My Lover, whose job was to help me open up, connect,
  receive love, and allow support in

My Risk Manager picked up strategies to protect me the best she knew how and had enormous influence over my actions, but she did not act alone.

All my other board members were on constant guard to steer me away from anything that could possibly lead me to emotional pain. They had their own costly tactics, and eating was just one of the strategies. If there was a chance I could get the message "You're not loved or good enough," the alarms would blaze, and the local bakery (only a stone's throw away) would come to my rescue.

What I discovered was I needed to work with all four board members to deeply heal the wounding message, "I'm not enough or loveable." I needed to uncover the wounding messages and change the inner dialogue. Until I worked with each part and got all four working together, I struggled.

Calling in the Troops

The first stop to transformation was my Risk Manager. Once she was updated and working in a more conscious way, she allowed the gateway to open for all the other board members. I was able to feel all my emotions in a safer way because I could finally work with the other parts.

I could embrace my anger, connect to my higher self, see healthy options more clearly, and nurture my little girl. With all the parts present and working, I could dive deeper into the healing of the underlying discomfort that led to my out-of-control eating.

"Great love and great achievements involve great risks."
– Dalai Lama

Beginning with the Risk Manager is a great place for you to start as well, so I included a powerful exercise below. You can use this exercise to connect with her and help bring her up-to-date.

Risk Manager Exercise

Remember, your Risk Manager is the assistant to the Magician. Even though you are about to dialogue with her, this is actually a Magician exercise. By separating parts out, like the part of the Risk Manager, and speaking to her, you get perspective. This detachment of parts is the power tool of the Magician, and it works!

It's a great journaling exercise, and if you write it all out, the insights you gain will amaze you. So grab a notebook.

You can also act it out loud using two chairs. You can sit in one chair "as you," and then talk to your Risk Manager in the other chair. Then, go sit in the other chair and be the Risk Manager.

Meet your Risk Manager:

You: Hello, Risk Manager, you're my protector. I'm curious … how long have you been in my life? Why did you appear in the first place? What was happening that made you feel the need to show up and give me strategies to help me?

(Be curious about its job and why it's in your life. Something happened to make it start watching out for you. For me, it was losing my dad. What's your protector's story, and why did it show up? Be as kind as you can be. Remember, it's working for you. It's protecting you. You may not like how it's doing its job now, but show some respect. It works hard for you!)

Risk Manager's Reply:

_____
_____
_____
_____
_____
_____

You: (Take some time to really hear it and understand why it has shown up in your life. Perhaps feel some gratitude for its service and tell it thank you for its efforts before you tell it how it's messing things up.

Then share with the Risk Manager the behavior that you don't like, tell it how it's hurting you, and ask it why it has you doing this behavior now. Some examples of self-sabotaging behaviors I hear people complain about often in my coaching practice are procrastination, lateness, overeating, overworking, cluttering, over-anything ... basically, anything that gets in the way of living the life you want.)

_____
_____
_____
_____
_____
_____
_____
_____
_____

Risk Manager's Reply:

_____
_____
_____
_____
_____
_____

You: (After hearing why it does what it does, share with your Risk Manager what you want from it now and how things have changed. Let it know you are a grown adult and that the risks are different now from those you had as a child. Bring it up to the present time, and see if you can negotiate some new strategies to keep you safe.

Let it know you are not firing it but that you need to tweak its job description. Let it know that you value its protection but that it might be over protecting you, and it can relax a bit. See if you can get it to step back a bit while you show it you have changed. It's been working so hard ... it must be exhausted. Let it know you will be talking with it for guidance, but you need a different relationship now.)

_____
_____
_____
_____
_____
_____
_____
_____
_____

Risk Manager's Reply:

_____
_____
_____
_____
_____
_____
_____
_____

Hopefully at this point you are having a lovely dialogue with your new best friend. It's been around for a long time, and you may need to have a few conversations with it until it can trust that things have indeed changed. Once you get it to see the very risks it has been trying to prevent are happening anyway, it should be able to reset a bit.

Keep trying to get it to see that you are an adult and the playing field has changed. Go back and forth until you think it can ease up a bit. If you have a stubborn Risk Manager, you may need to keep at it for a while until it can see the cost of its ways. You need to let it know you can handle your life and don't need the constant watching.

If you're still having difficulty, this is where having a Shadow Work® Coach can come in handy. Coaches are trained to get that smart Risk Manager to see with new eyes. For support, go to the resources page.

Here is a video demonstrating how to talk with your Risk Manager. I will show you the chair technique and guide you through this exercise.
Go to Junie's Transformation Toolbox
midlifeloveoutloud.com/toolbox

New and Improved Risk Manager

"Our society nurtures the illusion that all the rewards go to the people who are perfect. But many of us are finding out that trying to be perfect is costly."
– Debbie Ford

Thankfully, I now have a great relationship with my Risk Manager. One can say I have an updated Risk Manager working with my dated Risk Manager! My new Risk Manager, the one who's been brought up to speed, now knows I can handle things much better than when I was a kid.

She can spot the old one's tactics a mile away, and once she senses the unhealthy, over-controlling thinking popping up, my new one reminds the old one of the new tools I have. She grabs hold of her and slows her down before any real damage is done.

It's not that the old one is obsolete; she's just still in training not to be on high alert. I don't want her gone because she knows me so well. She's been around since the beginning when my needs were not being met and life school began. I want that protective radar scoping out danger. I also want her to relax a bit.

My old Risk Manager had me walking on eggshells, and I was so stressed out. Thank God for the updating. I can breathe easier, connect more deeply, and enjoy my life at a higher level.

The experience of losing my dad and the fear of losing love are humungous and can affect how I act with everyone, especially my partners. The difference now is when I feel the fear, I can allow it in without freaking out ... mostly! I still can feel anxious if I bump up against a loved one, but I handle it differently ... most of the time!

Gratitude for the Risk Manager

After seeing all your Risk Manager's strategies and the price you've paid because of its tactics, you might feel a bit pissed. I'm sure there were times you wished you had spoken up or had taken a risk of some sort and didn't. Your Risk Manager stopped you for one reason or another.

There were plenty of times I beat myself up because I wasn't showing up fully with my work. I was scared of falling flat on my face, so I played it small. That was my Risk Manager keeping me safe, but I didn't know it. All I knew was I felt like a failure and judged myself to be inferior.

I remember one of my clients being blown away once she realized the role her Risk Manager played in her life. She felt so alone and wanted a new relationship very badly. She had left an abusive relationship, and after some healing time, she felt she was ready to call in her new love, but she kept bumping up against her Risk Manager.

She was struggling. On the one hand, she wanted to say "yes" to love, but on the other hand, she felt paralyzed and incapable of getting back out there and saying to the world, "I'm ready!" Her Risk Manager knew she had experienced deep pain from the previous relationship and was working overtime to keep her from ever having that pain again.

Her Risk Manager told her very mean things to keep her from stepping out. Her self- talk was extremely negative, and she felt horrible. Feeling so insecure about herself kept her from taking steps to find her new love. She felt very lonely and was very sad.

Once her Risk Manager was able to see the strategies weren't working and that she was in pain, she began to listen. We got her to change course and work with her in a new way. My client also blessed her Risk Manager, thanking her for working so hard all these years.

It's a lovely thing when we truly can see we did our best, when we can accept our past choices and love ourselves, even if ultimately we got in our own way. There is deep healing. When we can see why we stopped ourselves—out of love—we can stop beating ourselves up and take a breath.

So if your Risk Manager's job is to keep an eye out for danger and she's worked hard to keep you safe all these years, perhaps you can give her a little loving? I know a part of you might be angry at her for some of the missed opportunities, but hopefully now you can see this part truly loves you.

Yes, she may have overshot and cost you some very important things in your life, but I invite you to see her dedication to keeping you safe all these years. It's quite beautiful, really.

-13-

How Relationships Can Suffer When the Board Isn't in Alignment

"Conflict avoidance is not the hallmark of a good relationship. On the contrary, it is a symptom of serious problems and poor communication."
– Henry B. Braiker

My marriage...

We were together for twenty years, and it wasn't always easy. There were a lot of great times, and there were times when we bumped heads like all married people do. With two egos and a spicy kid in the house, there were bound to be some challenges.

When my wasband and I clashed, it felt like the air was being sucked out of my lungs, and the alarms went blazing. I was so scared to bring up something controversial with my wasbund because there was a good chance we'd argue. Because of my childhood wounding, my Risk Manager would strategize how to keep my little girl from feeling unloved, and my Warrior would shut me down quickly to avoid the conflict altogether.

It wouldn't be a two-way disagreement either. It was more like he became sparked, and I headed for cover. I would try to get a word in edgewise to no avail and would give up. I felt unseen, unheard, and terribly unloved.

My Magician, with the help of her assistant the Risk Manager, did her best to prevent me from taking that risk of bringing up controversial subjects.

If the danger ensued, my Warrior stepped in and squashed my voice by making me retreat. I felt the anger, but because my Warrior was out of whack, she couldn't allow me to stand my ground. And, by not talking to my wasband, I didn't get the true connection I desired.

Building a wall around my heart and not sharing my truth were not conducive to creating intimacy. These strategies prevented the exact thing I wanted—deeper love and connection.

When I was younger and didn't have the tools that I acquired as an adult, this was a great strategy. As an adult, however, there was a cost. As a kid, not speaking up or acting in a way that could cause my parents to be angry with me worked. I didn't have the support or wisdom that I got in adulthood.

As kids, we have few choices and tools to get us by. We don't have access to our wise friends to confide in. We don't have a therapist to learn from. We don't have a community to rely on. We are vulnerable, and remember, when we are kids, our parents are gods to us.

The strategy that worked for me in the past took its toll on our marriage. Think about the consequences to your relationships if you don't communicate your needs or your truth. If a boundary is crossed, might it be healthy to express your anger in a clean, direct way?

If your Risk Manager is in protection mode and constantly telling you to stay quiet and to not rock the boat, how's that going to affect a relationship? She may keep you from conflict, but she also hinders true intimacy (into-me-see). If you're not sharing your truth, your heart, and your very essence, you are hiding your divine light from your beloved. Can you see how that could snuff out your life force? Not only are you inauthentic, you're not allowing your true love into your soul.

> *"Avoiding conflict to try to 'keep the peace' is a surefire way to gradually destroy your relationship."*
> – Geoff Laughton

If you're in a relationship and you're in your fear and can't access anger in a healthy way, the shit can really hit the fan. It's important to know when your boundaries have been crossed. It's important to be able to communicate cleanly to your loved one what happened and why you're angry. If you don't know how to embrace the energy cleanly, it comes out sideways, spilling blood.

It's not OK to hold your truth back and then come lashing out at your loved one like a wild animal, and it's certainly not OK to hate yourself; however, that's what happens. The anger can come inward like a boomerang and beat you up (more on shadowy anger in chapter sixteen).

Sometimes the result is not a bloodbath with your relationships, but a very sneaky Risk Manager skill called sarcasm. Do you know the definition for "sarcasm"?

"A sharp and often satirical utterance designed to cut or give pain"

When we hold back and don't express ourselves, who we really are, the energy will move in some way. It might be a full-blown explosion, or it might come out subtly as a joke that cuts to the core. That's not the best way to create intimacy!

Once I was able to see the value of accessing anger and truly allowing it into my consciousness, everything changed. I did a lot of

Shadow Work processes where I felt the anger and was able to see it for the powerful resource it is.

This is not to say I am uber comfy with anger; I just don't struggle with it anymore. I welcome it. I know it's my ally. It's not an invisible entity that takes over my body, making me attack the ones I love. And it doesn't attack me. I also don't find myself in a box of Oreo cookies to numb myself from the pain. I now know how to call upon my Warrior Self and have my sword at my side if I need to use it in a clean, direct way. It protects me.

In the past, it devoured me. When I stuffed down my emotions and held my tongue, my insides felt like they would explode, and there was nothing like a good binge to help that fear go down, which makes me think of the Mary Poppins song: "Just a spoonful of sugar helps the medicine go down." Well, it was massive spoonfuls of sugar, and it was medicine that numbed me as it went down. It numbed my voice, my truth, my pain, my fear … me.

Anger is Good?

I eventually learned that anger is not bad. In fact, it's a powerful energy that's extremely useful. How we manage the energy is what's important. It can be used in a harmful, mean-spirited, vicious way that hurts, or it can be harnessed and used in a way to express oneself in a healthy, direct, beautiful way that creates safety and intimacy. Who knew?

Now, most books stop here. They tell you that anger is good to own. Experts tell you to express yourself and not to hold back, that boundary setting and direct communication will create intimacy … but they don't tell you how.

So here is an exercise you can do right now to begin having a new relationship with your anger. As with all relationships, there are twists and turns, and sometimes we need to start over.

Here is your chance to start fresh and see anger in a whole new light. Chances are you have been pushing it away for so long that you wouldn't know it if you fell over it. Let's change that now!

You have to start somewhere, and this is a great place to begin … with a conversation.

Warrior Exercise

Before you start, I invite you to turn off your phone, stop doing anything that can distract you from being present, and create some solid, sacred time to meet your Warrior.

Imagine you are about to meet someone very important. Open your mind and allow yourself to get curious about him or her. Take a breath and get excited because you are about to understand and befriend a part of yourself that you might have disowned a long time ago.

You can do this as a journaling exercise, or you can actually take two chairs and move back and forth from one chair to another, speaking each part out loud. See the video for the Risk Manager in the toolbox if you need a refresher.

Use your own language.

You: Hello…

Warrior Response:

_____

_____

_____

_____

_____

You: Tell me, how long have you been in my life? When was the first time you showed up? How old was I? Who was there?

Warrior Response:

_____

_____

_____

_____

_____

You: Why did you show up? What was happening that made you show up?

Warrior Response:

_____

_____

_____

_____

_____

You: What is your job in my life? How do you serve me?

Warrior Response:

_____

_____

_____

_____

(You now have a chance to respond to how it serves you. Do you like how it shows up? Would you like it to behave differently? More present? Less present? Do its actions cost you something? Tell it how it affects you.)

Your Response:

_____
_____
_____
_____
_____
_____

(What is the Warrior's response to hearing about the cost?)

Warrior Response:

_____
_____
_____
_____
_____
_____

(Now dialogue with it back and forth for a while, telling it how you would like it to be.)

_____
_____
_____
_____
_____
_____

By the way, this exercise can be done with ALL your board members. You can speak to your Sovereign, Magician, and Lover, asking the same questions. You might be very surprised by the different answers you receive.

-14-

How the Board Works Together ... Not!

*"As you continue the work of acknowledging
and claiming the gifts of your past and standing
in the power of your present, you are freeing
up enormous reserves of creative energy."*
– Debbie Ford

My wasband and I are the best of friends now. Sometimes we laugh about those crazy days when we hit rough patches and my Magician with her comrade formulated over-the-top exit strategies. My Warrior was close by when the arguments ensued and held back my tongue, allowing the escape plan to begin.

My Sovereign was there too. She wanted me to have the dream relationship but was overshadowed by those other three board members. There was too much risk for my little girl! Trying to connect and rise up into the possibilities of success was not going to happen, and so the perfect escape route had to be implemented.

The Escape Route

There was a townhouse complex a few miles from where we lived. When my wasband began to share his fiery self, I mentally checked out and took a trip in my mind's eye to where I could live and how I could make money, and I told myself that I would be OK. I figured a townhouse was part of a community, so I wouldn't be alone. It also included maintenance, which meant the grounds would be maintained and if something broke, I'd be covered. Perfect plan.

I know ... it sounds a bit crazy, but that's what happens when your fear takes over and you think you'll die! Your Magician shows up to figure out how you'll survive, and this fantasy of moving helped me get through our bumps.

> *"Let fear be a counselor, not a jailer."*
> – Tony Robbins

We can get stuck in the fear of what might happen, but what if we had a skill set that enabled us to be seen and heard without feeling at risk? What if sharing your truth actually brought in more joy and deeper intimacy by virtue of opening up and revealing vulnerability?

We throw the baby out with the bathwater all the time in the name of keeping the peace. But when we keep the peace, are we really avoiding the pain, or are we avoiding the truth of the situation, which then opens us up to more hurt?

When you fail to share your truest expression of who you are, you create a wall of deception. You're not being fully you. Other people don't get to know the real you because you're hiding yourself. Is that what you want?

What a Mess!

At this point you can probably see the imbalance of my posse. My Magician and Risk Manager were in a panic, trying to keep me safe. My Warrior held back my tongue and made me retreat, which didn't allow me to take a stand and speak my truth. My Sovereign wasn't welcome because of the fear of not being good enough, which made her deflate and disappear. And my Lover ... well, she was raw and vulnerable, so she hid. She needed help and gave most of the power to the Magician to keep her safe.

A Work in Progress

> *"Your past does not equal your future."*
> – Tony Robbins

Here's a peek into how things have changed and what you can do to create a deeper connection with your partner. I still slip and fall, but things are quite different now. I have updated my programs and respond differently, though I'm still working out some of the kinks.

Last year, my boyfriend had a couple busy days, and I noticed he wasn't calling or texting. We'd been having some challenges, so I assumed he was triggered and was hiding in his cave. I was feeling extremely uncomfortable with his absence, so my old programming kicked in: I was feeling abandoned and alone.

I was experiencing pain, and I did do some things differently. I felt my aloneness. I let in my fear that he was mad at me and leaving me. I breathed. I connected to my Lover and asked for support from my Sovereign. I made sure my Risk Manager didn't put my head in the fridge to numb out. I also summoned my Magician who made me take a step back to look at what was happening before I invited my Warrior Self to make a move.

Even though I changed my strategies and allowed myself to feel my vulnerability and call upon my posse, I also made some poor choices. Old habits die hard...

My first mistake was assuming that my boyfriend had gone into his cave. I had no idea what was going on in his life, or if he was indeed hiding out. I jumped to conclusions. My dated Risk Manager still loves when I focus on others' inadequacies and not my own, so it was up to its old tricks. If I could judge him and decide he was the one not dealing with his discomfort, I didn't have to deal with mine!

Mistake number two occurred when I finally spoke with him. Instead of sharing what was happening inside me, I accused him of checking out; I put him in the wrong. It wasn't pretty, and it certainly didn't bring us closer.

If I had just expressed my sadness about his absence or shared that I feared him breaking up with me, or if I had harnessed the anger I had about him "forgetting" about me, I would have revealed my true self. I would have been more authentic. It probably would have brought us closer together.

Because of the old wiring, I was unable to be in the present, and I reverted to my old ways. I did do some things differently, but then I dropped the ball. I began making up stories to make him wrong, to keep me safe, and to not feel my pain.

I wanted more love and more connection, but instead, I threw up all over him, covering him with my judgment that he was not dealing with his emotions. Not only did I come across as the "know-it-all," pointing out his flaws (way to go, dated Risk Manager), I didn't get the closeness I truly wanted.

The cool new thing was that I spotted it. I owned my slip and apologized as soon as I saw that it was my fear taking me on a crazy road trip, that I had bought the ticket to the blame game. I was sad that I projected my fear onto him, and we moved on. Years ago, it would have been a complete mess, a big fight, followed by a shitload of cookies.

Making him out to be wrong seemed like a much better strategy than sharing my vulnerable self, but it backfired because I felt more alone and withdrew from my boyfriend. I didn't share what was in my heart, and attacking him put him on the defensive, which brought us deeper into conflict.

It took some work to get us back on track. We both were triggered, and we said things that hurt. We needed some breathing room. We had to slow down and truly listen to one another. Our Lover

Selves needed to feel safe enough to open up again. Once the pace changed, we could hear each other better, and our hearts opened.

As much as I've learned, I'm still practicing all the tools, and I don't always get it "right"! The key is staying awake and catching yourself when you slip before you fall down all the stairs.

One of the biggest things I practice is self-compassion. I'm human. I make mistakes. You make mistakes. Can that be OK? YES! It has to be OK, or there is suffering. This human journey is filled with lessons, and that usually includes tripping and falling. There will be bumps along the way because we're still learning.

May we continue to be open to the unfolding
May we continue to open our hearts
May we continue to have compassion for ourselves and others

The Ultimate Choice

Another point to consider is being right versus being happy. I can be stubborn, dig my heels in deeply, and be right, but that creates a wall between us. When I can step out of the right-and-wrong dynamic and choose to love, things really shift.

My updated Risk Manager had a big talk with my dated Risk Manager, reminding the dated Risk Manager of the great tools I have now and that I'm fifty-three, not fourteen! It needed to be reminded that there is safety in good communication and more risk in avoiding the controversy. That poor behavior could have cost me my relationship!

Shadow Work has taught me wonderful ways to communicate cleanly and effectively, creating more intimacy and reducing the risk of putting people on the defensive. I have taught my Risk Manager to let the Warrior do its job. Setting healthy boundaries is the way to go!

The Warrior gives us the ability to speak directly and own our truth. My Risk Manager needs to be reminded that the Warrior has my back and that there is a healthier, safer way to be.

The Skill I am Referring to is Clean Talk

The gist of this skill is this: Take responsibility for your feelings, get clear about the facts, own your judgments as judgments, and then ask for what you want moving forward. It doesn't have you pointing a finger and accusing anyone of doing something to you.

By owning your feelings and not making the other person wrong, it allows the other person to really hear you and know how you're affected by certain situations. This helps your partner truly see you and learn how you tick. It brings you closer.

It can also help you get clearer about what's going on with your outdated Risk Manager and how it's appeared once again!

When you feel hurt and make the other person responsible for your pain, they get defensive. That's why we use only feeling words like mad, glad, sad, fear, and shame. When you use words that end in "-ed," you are pointing a finger.

For example, if you say, "I feel attacked," you are basically saying they attacked you. Or if you say, "I felt abandoned," well, who might the abandoner be? Those are fightin' words. We all know that if someone is on the defensive, they can't hear you, so stick to the feeling words that are only about you. Feeling abandoned is not a true feeling.

If you're in a big reaction, chances are an old wound was poked. Give yourself a time-out. Get your Magician to see what's up. Allow yourself to feel what you need to feel, and own all of this as your experience.

If I notice I am triggered, I also reach out to my extended court, my Shadow Work colleagues. I ask for their help in seeing what I might be blind to seeing. Once I get a clear picture, I talk to my partner.

The skill of Clean Talk takes your relationships to new heights! (You can pick up a great CD at Shadowwork.com called Clean Talk to learn this great tool.)

A Quick Example of Clean Talk

I had a boyfriend that was chronically late. I'm not talking about ten or fifteen minutes late either, but hours late, without calling! Instead of attacking him for being late, I used this technique.

First, I took the time-out and went inward. Why was I upset? I needed to explore what was really happening inside me. I was mad because I judged his lack of communication and lateness as a sign that he didn't care about me. I felt unimportant. If I feel like I don't matter, I feel unloved.

After I processed, I told him that I was feeling angry (my feeling) when he showed up two hours late and didn't call (fact). My judgment was he didn't care about me and my time. That was my conclusion.

I didn't say, "You don't care about me or you would have called!" I could have also said that it seemed like other things were more important than me. This was my assessment. Then, I asked him to call me if he knew he was running late before he was late. I needed to know in advance so that I could act accordingly.

He was floored. He was used to a screaming ex-wife that made him wrong all the time. He was able to hear me and actually thanked me. He looked at me and said, "This is good. Wow, communication. This is really good." It was endearing. He had not experienced clean communication. Not only did I not make him the bad guy, which could have put him on the defensive, he actually felt safer to receive my truth in the future.

Even with Clean Talk, a person still might get defensive, but it will be a lot less volatile than getting in someone's face and saying, "You're always late and I don't like it!" With the Clean Talk model, the other person has time to reflect on the facts and the emotion they evoke, and they hear what happened inside their loved one, which hopefully makes them want to show up differently next time.

I usually catch myself before the blame game begins, but I'm still uncovering the old wiring from the tragic loss of my dad. The good news is I bounce back very quickly, and by getting really honest with myself and honoring my emotions, and with a good conversation with my Risk Manager, I can do some pretty quick damage control. Years ago, I didn't have the skills to see my avoidance techniques and would have had my orgy with Ben, Jerry, and all their other friends.

Clients often ask me, "Will the fear go away? Will my Risk Manager ever give me some space to be free? Will she step aside and let my other team players help me out?"

It's a journey, and yes, it will quiet down and give you some breathing room. The fear you will feel is one that will be your friend and will open you up to much better strategies. You can stop yourself much faster than in the past. What could have been years of self-sabotage might now be only moments or hours.

-15-

Messages Run Deep!

*"Most of us spend our lives protecting ourselves
from losses that have already happened."*
– Geneen Roth

As I said, my dad was my hero, my king, which meant I looked up to him and listened to everything he offered. The day he died, on some soul level he must have known it was his time, and through that entire day he gave me all the advice he could possibly give me to set me up for the rest of my life. One particular life lesson affected me on such a deep level that it still lingers a bit to this day.

He told me, "Don't gain weight because boys won't like you." How's that for a message?

Soon after his death, I began my love affair with food. It soothed my soul, but the weight gain also began. I think it was my way of never letting go of my dad. If he was right, that being fat meant men wouldn't want me, then it would be a great strategy to keep the door closed to other men. If I was overweight, I wouldn't have to replace my dad, and I could keep him on my pedestal forever.

Also, because I believed this message, there was suddenly great risk in trusting whether a man could accept me for me and truly love me. Not only was I afraid of losing him like I lost my dad, but what if I wasn't enough? What if he didn't see my unique light and could only see me as the unattractive fat girl?

The Proof He was Right and the Programming That I was Ugly

After my dad's death, both my culture and multiple encounters with boys supported this notion that having extra flesh meant I was ugly and that thin was beautiful. It seemed like my dad was right after all. Unless I looked a certain way, I would be unloved.

I remember one boyfriend in college telling me that if I lost some weight, I had a cute body under the fat! He really thought it was a compliment! I heard, "I'm fat, and if I'd only change, I'd be cute."

I had another college boyfriend leave me in the car to go into a friend's house to pick up something he had left there. I noticed I was in the car a very long time. It finally dawned on me: he hadn't invited me in because he was embarrassed by me. The belief I took on from that was "I don't fit the bill and am not beautiful." All his friends had tall, thin blondes for girlfriends, and I was not that.

Years later, he confirmed my suspicions, and he apologized for his warped perceptions. He too was programmed by what society fed him. He expressed anger that he too was a victim of the cultural programming, and it affected his relationships as well.

Not that this matters at all, but I wasn't even overweight back then. It didn't matter. I could've been tiny. The programming had been woven into my soul, and I felt shame about my body. I would look in the mirror and tell myself horrible things. The fear that I was not good enough was enormous.

Everywhere I looked I was being fed the message that unless I looked like the models, I was ugly. I was bombarded by the messages from our media that thin was beautiful, and if I had jiggly thighs, which I always did, I was unattractive. Everywhere I looked, I saw how I was supposed to look.

As time went on, I learned I was beautiful, and it didn't matter what shape or size body I was in. I met men that saw through the bullshit definition of what beauty looks like, and they were happy to praise my exquisiteness.

There was one particular man I never forgot because his message had an enormous impact on me and will live in my heart forever. I had been flirting with him for months at a dance club. We finally got on the dance floor and began doing the sexy dance—you know, where the man is behind you and his hands are on your hips and you move to the song together?

As we danced, he moved his hands from my hips to my belly. I quickly moved them back to my hips. He then moved them back to my belly. I felt extremely uncomfortable. His hands were on my fat. Here I was, excited to finally be dancing with him, and he was going to discover I was flawed and ugly.

So I took his hands and moved them right back to my hips. Maybe he didn't notice I was fat! He then stopped dancing and asked me why I kept moving his hands away from my belly. I was so embarrassed. I told him I was uncomfortable with my belly, and I joked that it was not my favorite part of my body. I held a lot of shame about my Buddha belly.

He put his hands back to my belly and said, "I love the whole package." Wow. He really meant it too. I could see how he adored me and saw me as this whole person. Here I was focusing on this one part I hated, and he was loving my whole being. He didn't see my belly roll as anything other than another beautiful part of me.

Could I ever see myself through those kinds of eyes? Could I actually love the whole package?

Many men complimented me through the years … I just didn't believe them. My lovers appreciated me, and I could see they were turned on sexually. I just didn't trust they were actually turned on by me, even though, intellectually, I believed they were into me and thought I was "all that" and even more. But at the end of the day, inside, I was terrified I wasn't enough.

I was always scared I would fall short in my lover's eyes, so all my board members had me on guard, which kept me from fully connecting with my partners. I was allowed just so much vulnerability.

With vulnerability came a great risk for criticism. I was terrified they would point out my flaws, and I'd be crushed. Each member had their influence and affected me. My council didn't allow me to risk being told, "If only you looked a certain way, you would be good enough." And so, I missed out on deep intimacy.

I'm not just talking about sex either. Yes, my mind would keep me from relaxing and receiving my lover's touch, but my overprotective mind kept me from deeply connecting emotionally as well.

Updating the Software

I'm happy to say that when I met my wasband in 1990, he began dismantling the old programming. He saw me as hot and beautiful, and I mostly believed him. The problem was the old wounding messages ran deeply. I could see he was attracted to me, but I was terrified to truly let him in. My board could let me trust him only up to a point.

The old programming had me "shoulding" on myself all the time.

I should be thinner.
I should be fitter.
I should be anything other than me!

How could he find me sexy when I have fat thighs?

More healing had to happen, and that's where Shadow Work came in. It took me to a new level of loving myself and trusting that not only am I beautiful, but it also doesn't matter what others think.

> *"When divine consciousness enters, the shift occurs and*
> *you will be engulfed by what will feel like the greatest*
> *love imaginable – a love in which your soul realigns*
> *with your spirit and they meet together as one."*
> – Debbie Ford

Exercise:
A True Blessing ...
Deepening the relationship to your
Sovereign and Lover

For this exercise, grab your phone or some other recording device. Get some tissues because tears may flow. Also, get a pillow and a blanket. Find a quiet place where you won't be interrupted. I invite you to create some sacred time for yourself. I want you to experience this process AND have time to allow it to sink in before you run to get dinner ready!

This is an opportunity to connect with the part of you that KNOWS how valuable and beautiful you are and to feel the vulnerable self who needs support. Now, you may think, "That's the problem! I don't know how awesome I am! I think I'm ugly, fat, and no one will love me." I'm telling you, that's the part that will receive the blessing!

So take a moment and ask yourself, "Who or what knows the truth? Who can hold this vulnerable self and bless them?" This one will have the energy of the Sovereign.

Is there someone in your life who has had your back and told you how special you are? For this exercise, maybe you would like to invite an angel or other divine part to visit? You can even choose to create an ideal figure like an ideal mom or dad, a parent who can tell you the things you needed to hear and didn't. Think about someone who can hold this little girl (or boy) and bless her. The little girl is the Lover Self.

Start the recording.

Sit on the pillow and take a moment to feel your sadness. Allow yourself to hear the negative self-talk that makes you feel insecure or powerless. I want you to become the part of yourself that hurts. Feel it. When you can really connect to the vulnerability, switch places with the blessing part.

Take the pillow in your arms and hold this pillow as if it were the little girl. See her in front of you. See her as the young child who got the messages when she was young that she wasn't good enough or that she was a bad little girl. Whatever her messages, see this little girl before you through your loving eyes and bless her.

What does she need to hear? What can you tell her, from this place of knowing, that will help her see that she is a divine being of light?

If you chose an ideal mom or dad, what does your little girl need to hear? What would she have loved to have heard but didn't? Tell her what you see in her—her gifts, her loving heart, her sweetness. Give her new messages. Let her know she is loved.

When you have said everything she needed to hear, switch places. Grab the recording, rewind, and then play when ready. Sit back on the pillow, go back into the vulnerable Lover Self, wrap the blanket around you as if the arms of the Sovereign One were wrapped around you, and feel her holding you. Now listen to this blessing. Take it in. Breathe it in. This is your Sovereign Self blessing your Little Girl, the Lover.

-16-

Oh Warrior, Where Art Thou?

"You are imperfect. Permanently and inevitably
flawed. And you are beautiful."
– Amy Bloom

So where was my Warrior when I needed protection from the mean-spirited comments? Why didn't I stand up for myself and set good, healthy boundaries with anyone who said boo to me?

One would think the terrible things men told me would have made me angry and that my Warrior Self would have stood up and said, "Fuck you!"

That didn't happen because I was scared of anger. Anger was there, but I didn't know how to access it. I didn't know how to get my Warrior working in a good way, so it was suppressed.

Where, Oh Where, Did My Warrior Go?

When I was twelve years old, there was no internet, which meant YouTube didn't exist. I was listening to the radio when suddenly a song that, I loved that I had heard in a movie once, started playing. It was "Time in a Bottle" by Jim Croce.

There it was, the song I thought I would never hear again, and just as I was celebrating, my brother changed the station and it was gone. GONE! I was pissed and said, "Shit!" just as my dad walked by my bedroom door. He stopped, looked at me with such judgment, and said, "Is that how I raised you?" His response rocked me to my core.

Recently, my mom told me something I didn't know about my dad. She said he hated cursing. Looking back at this story, it makes even more sense now. I had done the very thing he despised. No wonder I received his disgusted tone and a look that was nothing less than an arrow through my heart.

It was one of the worst moments in my life. I had never been anything less than perfect for him. Of course, that's wiring in itself. I thought I had to be perfect or I would lose his love. I always was the ideal little girl he could be proud of.

My cursing disappointed my dad, and this scenario happened because my anger leaked out and then my dad got angry at me.

The lesson was loud and clear: anger had high consequences that I never wanted to experience. By yelling at my brother, I got the critical eye from my dad. When I felt his disapproval, I felt shame. I needed to be more careful, so my Risk Manager kicked in and reprimanded my Warrior for acting up and causing a scene.

I now know anger is an amazing asset, and life has changed for me now that I have embraced its energy. Healthy anger is a gift! Until I experienced Shadow Work, however, anger had no place in my life.

After that episode with my dad, I cut anger out of my life like a horrible tumor. My Magician had witnessed this whole transaction and decided that anger was dangerous. She then gave the Warrior the task of holding my tongue. That's why my Warrior squashed my voice with my wasband. These two were in cahoots to keep me from ever feeling that horrible judgment again.

I took on the belief that expressing anger would make things worse and cause more separation, that people would get hurt, and I wouldn't feel loved.

Where Does the Energy Go?

Instead of taking a stand and speaking up for myself, the anger went inward. I would tell myself that I was the one to blame. I was the fat one. I was the flawed one.

I also think on some unconscious level I believed it was better to hurt myself than someone else—nice in theory, but really? Why should anyone suffer? But suffer I did. If I felt anger creep up, I would put out the fire as fast as I could. I would never want anyone to feel the brunt of that dark, evil energy.

It's Everywhere!

Because I disowned my own anger (or at least tried to make it disappear) and saw it as a terrible quality, I would sniff it out in others. I saw this especially with my wasband, and man, did I judge him harshly for being angry.

That's what happens when we squash an aspect of who we are and throw it in the shadow bag. The bag isn't completely sealed. It leaks, and we see the "bad" quality everywhere we go in others, and then we judge them! We call that projection.

I'm not saying that they're not behaving poorly, but judging others' behavior is a clue that there is a shadow lurking inside you, screaming to be seen and expressed. Think of that saying, "When you point a finger at someone, three fingers are pointing back at you." In AA, they say, "If you spot it, you got it." Well, that which you judge in others is within you as well.

Remember the shadow exercise earlier in the book? What you despise in others is your projection of the very quality that is within you that you disowned.

Because of this, my wise Magician was on high alert for the evil expression of anger. Since she labeled it as a terrible quality to possess, I did everything I could to stay away from it, to not feel it, and certainly to not express it. That was my wiring about anger, so you can see why I would never want to be that!

I Put My Anger in Shadow

"There's nothing wrong with anger
provided you use it constructively."
– Wayne Dyer

I decided I would never express my anger. I wouldn't dare make someone else feel so judged and alone. I didn't want to express my anger out of fear that I would alienate the very people I wanted to connect with in life.

When we deny a part of us, like the energy of anger, it doesn't just disappear. It's energy, and it needs to move, so it comes out in other ways. It comes out sideways. It comes out as flash anger. It spews out at the ones we love when we least expect it, or it comes inward and hurts us.

Like it or not, the Warrior is a valued member of the board; it's a powerful energy. It needs to be expressed, or it will be a disgruntled employee and act out! Once a board member, always a board member, and I needed to learn how to work with it, or there would be a price to pay.

Years ago, before my inner transformation, my anger would spill out unexpectedly. By pushing down my anger and not handling my emotions, the energy would build up and, like a volcano, it would blow. It's amazing my wasband's beard survived the spewing molten lava!

I did my best to control it, but that energy was gonna move one way or another. If I wasn't raging at my wasband, I was raging at myself.

I would look in the mirror and tell myself things like:
"I'm a fat pig. No one will love me or want me!"
"I'm disgusting."
"I'm weak and pathetic."

By turning my anger inward, I beat myself up, but it kept me from the other battles. Again, it was a good strategy when I was younger, when I didn't have support, but as the years went on, that anger increased and a bonfire brewed deep inside me. By not dealing with the underlying programming, I suffered greatly.

If a conflict arose (and unless you live under a rock, it's bound to happen), I would get so scared that my little girl would tremble. The sword was now turned inward and became vicious. My inner dialogue went something like this:
"Damn, I screwed up again"
"He's so angry with me. He must not love me."
"I must be very bad, otherwise he wouldn't be so mean!"
"Something must be very wrong with me!"
"I'm just not _____ enough."

I would tell myself, "If he really loved me, why would he ever get angry?"

Once I reclaimed my Warrior, the inner abuse lessened, and more balance was restored.

Then and Now

Here's an example of how things are now after the long, winding journey of welcoming my cast of characters into my life:

Last year, my boyfriend and I bumped up against each other. We were new to the relationship and were still getting to know each other. We were madly in love, but then the huge pothole in our newly paved road appeared, and we fell into it.

We both had brought some baggage to the party and were learning how to navigate each other's territory. As much as we were enjoying the sweetness, there was a moment that was less than ideal, and we both got triggered.

My mom had just fallen and needed surgery. I was feeling some fear and very vulnerable. He is very intuitive and spotted my need for support. It was a great conversation.

He was present and loving. I was able to open up and share what I was feeling. I felt really heard and held, but then I said something that didn't quite come out the way I intended, and he got mad, which was kind of the perfect storm.

The last thing I needed was for him to be angry. I was feeling vulnerable and needed love and then boom! It got messy. Energetically it felt like he left me. I felt my fear of abandonment rise up, and I reacted.

Calling in My Court

First, my Lover:

My little girl was very sad and needed a hug. I felt the separation occurring, and that was the last thing she needed. I looked at him and practically begged him not to be mad, but he was triggered. No hugs for me, just a reprimand.

I have to say that this was not a well-thought-out plan, letting my little girl out of the gate first. I was already feeling vulnerable. My Magician or Warrior would have been a much better place to start.

I had hoped that when he heard my plea for understanding, he would melt and come back to the moment. Then it was obvious— he was long gone. I had stepped on a very raw, old toe, and he was not going to back down.

My Warrior and Magician kicked in pretty quickly to rescue my little girl. I did my best to put out the fire, but the fire was there and there was no turning back. My Magician tried to reason with him, but he couldn't hear me.

Then my anger appeared, and my Warrior realized this wasn't a safe place to hang out. I took a stand and chose to leave the conversation, which was different from the past, when my Warrior made me run for the hills with my tail between my legs.

My Warrior got me out of Dodge because Dodge was burning down. I actually felt powerful when I said, "No more!" One might think this was similar to the past, but energetically it was completely different. I didn't cut his head off or spew the flames, nor did I check out.

In the past, I would have done anything to stop the argument ASAP. I wouldn't have wanted to risk losing the relationship or, worse yet, have a fight. I would have apologized immediately, and my Warrior would have had me sweep it under the rug.

This time, I said what I needed to say and set the healthy boundary. I was unhappy that this transpired, but I also felt clean with my words and actions.

I took great care of my little girl. I reached out for support from my friends who knew what was happening in my life. I gave myself some time to process what had transpired with him, and then, when I was ready, I used Clean Talk to share what happened inside me.

Now, did he drop the ball? I mean, I did tell him I was having a rough day.

Here's the thing: your happiness is not contingent on others' actions or reactions. Yes, he was not showing up the way I needed, but it was my need and my story that I needed to look at.

I needed to tell him what happened so that he could then understand me better and hopefully take responsibility for the ball dropping, if indeed he dropped it.

Maybe I was uber vulnerable and made a mountain out of molehill. Who knows? With Clean Talk, I did what I could to communicate what happened to me, hoping for a healthy resolution, which eventually came.

-17-

The Body Never Lies...

*"The moment you change your perception, is the
moment you rewrite the chemistry of your body."*
– Dr. Bruce Lipton

Just as emotions are to be embraced and welcomed, illness can be a powerful doorway to deeper understanding and healing. When we experience disease, our first thought is usually, "How can I get rid of it as fast as I can?" Makes sense, right? Pain sucks, so why wouldn't we want to move it along?

Sickness is just another great opportunity that gets offered to us while we walk this human path. If we choose to allow it in and welcome it, there is much wisdom to be gleaned. Sadly, we often see the body for just the body and don't realize there are messages being sent.

My Pain Saga Continues

Recently I was plagued with hip and back pain that went on for months. When it first showed up, I thought it would be a piece of cake for me to process and get it to leave quickly. With all I knew about mind-body wellness, healing, and the techniques for things like this, I was quite sure its days were numbered as soon as it began.

That was not the case. I was a bit arrogant—or maybe just naïve (I think both)—to think it would be a walk in the park. All I knew was that I wanted it gone!

I kept asking myself for the lesson. I knew the pain was there for a purpose, and I was grateful that I knew that, so I kept at it to get to the bottom of this very annoying pain. I believe all things happen for us, not to us.

To me, there is a divine plan, and when life throws me a curveball, it's moving me in a direction for a certain outcome. I believe my soul signed up for a certain set of circumstances, and the path I'm on is designed perfectly for me.

Even though I believed all that, I was also so frustrated! The pain took its sweet time to let me in on the reason it was in my life and hurting me. Sometimes we find ourselves in a dark tunnel and can't see the light until we get closer to the doorway. I was stuck and had no clue when the light would appear!

I did all the right things, but it lingered on.

I really thought I had this. I knew how to handle pain. I'm a shadow worker and know the power of the mind as well as its tricks. I do processes all the time with my clients, helping them get to the root cause of their pain and then helping them release it. I had done it multiple times for myself with the numerous emotional release techniques I knew, so I thought it would be easy-peasy for me this time.

"Healing is not an overnight process, it is a daily cleansing of pain, it is a daily healing of your life."
– Leon Brown

But the pain would not go. It hung in there. I would get better, but then it would change and new symptoms arose. It was like chasing a wild animal. It kept showing up, then went running fast to another location, only to hide again and show up somewhere else.

It was making me crazy and very uncomfortable. I would think I was headed to the finish line only to find myself with another sleepless night of discomfort. It began to take a toll on me.

I got really angry at how long the healing process was taking. Intellectually I knew it was my teacher. I knew the pain had gifts for me. I thought I knew so much about healing this kind of thing, and yet it wasn't leaving. It was an unwanted guest that overstayed its welcome.

"Pain is a great teacher of mankind.
Beneath its breath, souls develop."
– Marie Von Ebner-Eschenbach

I did all I could to get rid of it. I ate well. I went to my chiropractor, my acupuncturist, and my massage therapist. I searched inwardly for "why" I had it and dove into some powerful transformative processes, but it would not ease up.

It held on. It was a deep, nagging, unforgiving pain.

It had been at least a dozen years since I had experienced pain like this. It used to keep me in bed for days, but once I learned Shadow Work and how to honor the pain, how to go in and learn from it and receive the lesson, it would leave. This time, none of my healing tools were working.

I dove into my anger and released it, but no go. I opened up my heart and sobbed, but still, the pain lingered on. It brought me to my knees.

Finally, I heard myself say, "I don't know what to do!" Bingo. There it was. My vulnerability. My fear. Then I truly began the healing work.

It's not that what I did up to this point was moot. In fact, I believe all the processing helped me get to this vulnerable place. Shadow Work can be like that. It opened me up and revealed the layers that needed to be shed to get to this place of deep vulnerability. I wasn't ready yet to see and feel the true issue at heart.

My Risk Manager was hard at work once again, stopping me from going to the deepest pain. After months of struggling and processing and jumping around from one practitioner to another and one Shadow Work process to another, I finally realized where I had to go to get to the heart of this illness.

It's not like I didn't do my work before this moment. I pulled apart what I could see. I was on a mission to move this baby out of my body.

I tapped into my Warrior and felt the anger and ran with it.
I welcomed my Lover, opened my heart, and melted as the sobs flowed.
I invited my Sovereign in to support my sweet little girl who felt like mush, and it picked me up and breathed new life into my soul.
I also had my Magician online, and it looked at my fear head-on.
I did some transformative processes from all directions with what was bubbling up in my conscious mind, but I was just getting warmed up.

There were things in my life that felt overwhelming and scary, so that's the work that appeared. It made sense. I put out the different parts, which led me to some very powerful releasing work. I also did an awesome process where I had my pain be a part, and we had a long conversation.

I asked it why it was there, what was it trying to teach me, and how might I negotiate with it so it didn't need to work so hard. I learned a lot from talking to it. It's sort of like talking to the Risk Manager.

By understanding its strategies and why it's doing the job it does, we can then change things up.

I kept at it, learning and growing and following the path this pain was leading me on, but it still lingered until that moment when I heard myself say, "I don't know what to do!" Then I knew. This was about my son.

How Vulnerable Can I Get?

As I share this next piece, I invite you to ask yourself some of the same questions if you also suffer from some physical challenge. Go into your pain and see what it has to say to you. Describe your pain. How does it feel? How does it affect your life? Then ask, what else does that describe for you in your life?

As I heard myself say that I didn't know what to do about the nagging, uncomfortable, never-ending, confusing, exhausting pain, I then asked, "What else confuses me in my life to the point that I don't know what to do? What is nagging, uncomfortable, painful, never-ending, confusing, and overall exhausting?" I then knew why I had this pain.

I don't usually share this part of my life because it's such a difficult story to explain and quite heart-wrenching. I often hear, "Oh my God! How can you ever be happy when you're experiencing such a terrible thing in your life?" That's one of the gifts of the Shadow Work and my spiritual walk: I can feel joy in spite of the circumstances.

For the purposes of this book and to help you understand how illness can open up a doorway to help you heal, I find I must go into this part of my life as an offering to you.

My Greatest Pain

In 2012, with my blessing and for good reasons, my son flew the coop. He was sixteen years old. He got his GED and headed out into the world to become the adult he had wanted to be since he took his first breath.

When I say "out into the world," I mean he moved 1,000 miles away! He got a job soon out the gate and was well on his way to proving he could make it on his own. He was also on a mission to prove he didn't need any help from anyone and that he would be fine.

I knew he would be fine. I knew he was more capable than most adults and would not only survive but thrive. However, I had to work to convince his dad that he was good to go.

It was a bit tough to get his dad on board because he had not seen or spoken to him for over a year. My kid had chosen to lock him out of his life, so his dad didn't quite know what to make of this very unusual request. After a while, his dad saw the writing on the wall and agreed it was time to let him go. He saw it was best for all parties involved.

What I didn't know was once my son left, I would not hear from him or see him again. For no reason that makes any sense to me, he cut me out of his life. He had done this to his dad the year before, but to me? It blew my mind and certainly broke my heart.

Obviously, there is a long story and lots of details, but for the purpose of this book, let's keep it simple and just say my heart aches and there are days that are very hard. I pray every day for him to reach out again to me, but for almost five years now, I have not had my son in my life.

You might ask, "What could you have possibly done to deserve this behavior from your son?" You might wonder if I have reached out to him, tried to connect or ask for forgiveness—anything to rectify this very sad situation. I have done it all, and at the end of the day, the story doesn't really matter.

I will say that when my head hits the pillow each night, I know my side of the street is clean and I have done everything I could possibly do through the years to be a great mom and make things right now.

Being right, however, doesn't matter. I can have everyone tell me it isn't my fault and I was a great mom, but the fact is, I don't have my son in my life right now, and it hurts. He's still gone, and it tears at my soul.

The good news is that I know he is OK. He speaks with his dad, and he is safe and doing well. As for the rest, I am quite in the dark.

I have my spiritual beliefs that remind me we all have our life's journey, and he is on his as I am on mine; that doesn't change the fact that I don't have him. I don't get to hear his day-in and day-out adventures. I don't get to see him grow into the man he is becoming. Even if I think I did nothing wrong and that I'm in the right, it doesn't matter. Right, wrong, or in between, he's gone.

I truly believe all is in divine order, and we're exactly where we need to be for our soul's journey, but I'm also a human being—a mom with a beating heart—and I grieve my son's absence.

My Magician is strong and offers great perspective, reminding me the only thing that's bad right now is the meaning I give to this absence of my son. If my story is I am abandoned and left out from his life, I hurt. If my thought is he is fine, he is living his life on his terms and doing well, then I have way more peace.

It's great when my Magician is present because I have perspective. I remind myself he is well and living his life. It's awesome when my Warrior is there and I feel grounded, strong, and able to set good, healthy boundaries around my heart. I'm thankful for my Sovereign Self who offers me the blessing of what a great mom I was and gives me hope for a happy ending. It's even great when my Lover shows up and the tears flow because I feel the loss and it connects me to the love I feel for him.

I try to focus on what is good, but I miss him terribly. I wonder what his life is like. I wish I could hear his voice and share this part of his life with him. I think about the years I've missed and wonder if I will ever get to hear his voice again. All these thoughts sting...

"Where focus goes, energy flows."
– Tony Robbins

I do my best to track my thoughts and stay positive. I focus on the fact that the story isn't over and Spirit is working. I do slip and fall and find myself in my grief. I do my best to keep my mind clear of the worrying, grieving "mom thoughts" because they take me out of my present life and get in my way of living fully now.

Intellectually, I see clearly. I trust Spirit to take care of my son. I trust in the soul's journey, and that all is perfect as is, but I am engulfed with emotions, and my thinking can only take me so far.

Back to the Back Pain

I asked myself what was ongoing, painful, confusing, exhausting, and nagging that just wouldn't go away. You guessed it, this situation with my son. I tell myself I must move on. I tell myself all is well and I need to focus on what I can do, not what I can't. I live each day as fully as I can, but in the background of my mind is the terrible loss.

"By itself, conscious positive thinking cannot overcome subconscious negative feelings."
– Joe Dispenza

Such a small part of our mind runs our life show. We think our conscious mind is steering our choices, but in actuality, most of our decisions are made by our subconscious mind. We have picked up powerful programming from our past experiences that makes us act and feel as we do.

We have access to only a small part of our brain—the conscious part—even though most of our brain is subconscious. Until we change the mapping of the subconscious programming, we are incapable of creating the empowered, happy life we strive to live. We are running blindly while trying to think our way to success.

I use my conscious mind to think my way through my son's loss, focus on the positive, and trust that Spirit has my back, but subconsciously, a lot is still brewing that needs to be addressed.

I could display my vision board proudly and scatter affirmations around the house, reminding me of what I want to invite into my life, but that plays only a very small part in my day-to-day experiences.

I felt abandoned, betrayed, angry, scared, and every other emotion a mom could feel after a child leaves. I had old beliefs linked to the present circumstances, and I had to dive deeper past the conscious mind.

I had more to heal. There was a much more painful layer to touch on and transform before this pain was to leave. I thought it was about being overwhelmed by my new relationship and the stress of my business. Yes, those things were present, but it was the beginning of the road that led me to the underbelly of the pain ... the loss of my son.

I needed to go into the wound of loss.

> *"There's nothing like a little physical pain to keep*
> *your mind off your emotional problems."*
> – Dr. John Sarno

Years ago, I bought a great book by Dr. John Sarno called Healing Back Pain. The crazy thing was it had been on my shelf for the longest time, and for whatever reason, I never read it.

I had been struggling with hip pain, and it wasn't responding to my healing protocol. Because I was at a loss as to what to do, I was finally drawn to read it.

As I read the book, it all made sense. In addition to loving what he wrote, I also discovered he was located in NYC, so I called to set up an appointment with him. I needed his help. I had had this pain 24/7 for a couple months, and after acupuncture and massage, it wasn't going away. I was shocked when he himself called me back.

We spoke for about forty-five minutes. Ultimately, after I explained my symptoms and that my MRI showed herniations and other nasty deteriorations in my spine, he said, "Hogwash!" He told me there was nothing wrong with me! Herniations are like gray hair on the spine.

He explained that getting a gray hair doesn't mean your head is going to hurt; it's a normal condition. My pain was my brain distracting me from something in my life. I needed to look at what I was repressing and deal with my life. Whoa!

I fully believed him. There was nothing wrong with me! I had been feeling a lot of anger and unrest in my marriage and stress with my kid, so after our phone call I had a big cry. It was more like a deep dry heave from the depths of my being. Ancient tears, old and dark and ugly.

The next morning, my pain was gone! Seriously! After months of 24/7 pain, I had nothing. I knew then in every cell of my being that unexpressed feelings hurt us and the mind and body are connected deeply. I also knew life was changed forever for me. If my back hurt, it was a wake-up call to look at something I wasn't dealing with. It was my body speaking to me. It was at this point I began my deep personal-growth work.

Dr. Sarno had spoken to me about the strategies our brains use to keep us from feeling pain. I believe he was speaking about our very smart Risk Manager who is hard at work to keep us safe. When we sense emotional danger is about to rear its ugly head, we distract ourselves. Science demonstrates the physiology of this occurrence. The Risk Manager is the part that makes this happen.

The Shadow Work model fit perfectly with what Dr. Sarno explained. I now had not only resources to help me access the hidden beliefs and old wiring from the past that caused my disease, but also tools to shine a light on my current situation.

Things brew in our subconscious. If we don't process these feelings, we will react in some unhealthy way. In this situation for me, it was the repressed emotions around my son's absence.

Shadow Work is an amazing body of work, and it helped me with this unrelenting back pain.

Let's Talk Baseball

I think Shadow Work is a lot like baseball. You want to score. You want the process to be a home run. Whether your pain is physical or emotional, you want your process to hit it out of the park—boom—and be done with it.

You want to get to home base as soon as possible. You wish you could just go directly home, but you have to go around the bases, hit each one, until you get to home plate.

Sometimes you get a home run! You get the big hit and it's done. Other times it's a bit slower. You linger on first. You slide into second and then dive into third before you get the opportunity to score.

This was one of those times for me.

I had to go to each base, feel it, digest it, and then when I was ready, run to the next. I kept hoping each process would be the perfect hit, but it was a slow journey to home base.

I wanted my pain to leave. I pushed and screamed and pleaded and cried, hoping to get to the truth of my issue, but in the end, I had to do each step, unfolding my way to the real home base of my truth. I know my Risk Manager was preventing me from going too quickly to home plate. This was a big deal, and my Risk Manager knew it. So I went very slowly.

First Base:

I had a conversation with my pain to find out what was happening. I truly believe my Risk Manager was calling the shots, so it threw me a curve ball and made me focus on my work, not my son. All good. It was first base, and it was warming me up for the long haul.

The Conversation Went Like This:

Me: So, pain, you've been with me since last summer. You're constant, nagging, limiting, and I really need you to go. You're in my way. You're hurting me and keeping me from enjoying my life. Why are you here? What's your purpose?

Pain: I need you to slow down. You're all over the map. You keep adding new marketing strategies to your business and are not following through. You're too scattered, and you need to hunker down. If I keep you in one place, you'll focus.

(Ouch. It knows me so well. The pain made sense. Yes, I'd been a bit scattered. I had moved to a new town and had not really gotten myself into a good routine. My coaching practice was dwindling because I stopped promoting it, and I also began a new relationship.

There was a lot of life happening for me and I was enjoying it, but I was also frustrated because I was in pain. I had to let the pain know it was hurting me and try to get it to let go a bit.)

Me: Yes, that's true. I'm still getting my bearings, and there's a lot of new navigating. I chose earlier in the year to focus on my book and film so my practice took a hit, but I'm slowly getting back on track. I'm in love and want to put time and energy into this new relationship too.

So yes, I have a lot going on, but I need you to back off. I hear you're trying to get me to focus, but all you're doing is making me angry and scared, which is not helping me focus. In fact, I am jumping around to different practitioners for help, spending a fortune, and I'm not exercising because of the pain. You're stopping me from moving forward. Do you see how your tactics are backfiring?

Pain: I can see that, yes, but how else can I get you to start focusing on your work?

(OK, so here, you see that my pain wants to help me. It has good intentions. It's just doing it in a way that has a cost, literally and figuratively. Once it sees that it's not really working the way it thought it would, it's open to suggestions—at least I hope it is!)

Me: Well, firstly, I see you're trying to get me to work more and settle down. Thank you for trying to slow me down so I can achieve more in my career. I need less pain. I want to get back to the gym. When I exercise, I feel better, have more energy, and can work more. If I'm in pain, I don't work out and then I feel sluggish. Can you ease up a bit?

Pain: Well, I'm glad you see my intention was to help. I see now the strategy isn't working the way I planned. So, if you exercise, you will feel better and work more?

Me: Yes.

Pain: How do I know you'll do that? You've said you were going to the gym before and then slacked off.

(This is where you get to negotiate with your pain. I began by telling the pain what my needs were and what I was willing to do. The pain then questioned whether I really would follow though. I said, "Give me less pain, and I will commit to an exercise routine."

The conversation went on for a bit. By the end of it, the pain said it would ease up and see if I indeed followed through. It also said I needed some accountability and asked what I would do to get more work done. I spoke to my friend who also works at home about co-working. We now meet weekly and get our work done.

Remember, this was first base. It helped. My pain definitely eased up, but it lingered, so I needed to do another process.)

Exercise:
Understanding your pain

This is another Magician exercise. It gives you more perspective on why you have your disease. When you utilize the Magician's keen eye, you can see new options. With new options come new awareness and choices. Both can lead you to deeper healing.

You can use some of the questions I used above with your illness.
Get two chairs. One is for you. One is for the voice of the pain.
Sit in one chair, look at the other one, and ask it the first question. Why are you here?
Then go sit in the other chair, the chair of the disease, and let it speak to you. Really listen to what it has to say. You may be surprised by why it's in your life. Hopefully you will glean some clarity, which might be all you need for some healing.

It helps to have a coach facilitate you, but just asking some of these questions can make a great difference.

Go to midlifeloveoutloud.com/toolbox to access Junie's Transformation Toolbox. I'll demonstrate this process with pain and guide you with this exploration.

Second Base:

I was feeling overwhelmed and scared. I had just signed the contract to write this book. My practice was quiet, and my bank account was dwindling. I wasn't focused, and my hip pain kept me from exercising so my energy was low.

I began to really freak out, wondering if I had it in me to follow through and get this book done. It had been months of no significant pain relief, and I was worried.

The next process I did was a Warrior piece.

First, I looked at the voice that was judging me. It told me I was going to fail. It said I had wasted time and money building this new coaching career and asked who I thought I was to write a book!

If you whittle down the message, you get:
You're not good enough!
You're going to fail!
Who do you think you are?!!!!

The first thing you need to do is look at where these thoughts come from. If I wasn't born with the thought that I wasn't good enough, then where did I pick this up and who is this judging person?

I saw that it was leftover memories from my days being bullied. It was my nemesis from childhood squashing my light and making me feel inadequate.

This voice took away my power, making me feel small and frightened. It had me questioning whether I could do it. This part was beating me up and making me want to hide under the covers and disappear.

Well, my pain was doing a great job at that, making me stay home instead of going to the gym. It had me cancel plans with friends and literally stay in bed. The bullying voice was causing me to shrink, and the pain was the perfect manifestation to keep me from being seen.

I knew that I had to stand up to this voice and hold my ground or I would never accomplish my goals. I also thought, "Great! Let me feel my Warrior's strength and set this boundary, and I'm bound to get some pain relief!"

I put this message out on the carpet and confronted it. It was great! I let this part know I was more than enough and more than capable to get this done. I felt my inner strength and chopped this voice into little pieces until it was inaudible. Wahoo. I won and felt the energy of my healthy Warrior.

My pain got better—but just a tad. I was so frustrated that there was something more to work on. I was still not getting to home plate.

Would you like to feel the strength of your Warrior? I created a video demonstrating a quick technique that helps you access the power within!
Go to midlifeloveoutloud.com/toolbox for Junie's Transformation Toolbox.

Third Base:

This was a continuation from second base. Even though the Warrior had set the boundary with the bullying voice, the part was still there making me feel small and wanting to hide. The small part, my nine-year-old little girl, felt scared and hurt.

It was time for my Sovereign to hold and bless my little girl. Remember the exercise you did in chapter fifteen with the Sovereign blessing the Lover? That's what I did.

My Sovereign held my vulnerable self and said, "You are more than enough. The voice you hear that scares you isn't true. What is true is you're a gift.

"Not only do you have what it takes to finish the book, but by sharing your truth, your heart, and your love, people will learn that healing is possible, and that is a great service. This is your path. This is your soul contract. You are here for a reason, and that is to share your authentic self.

"You are not alone, you are loved, and if you feel scared or alone, feel me. I am here for you. You can also seek out more support from your friends and colleagues. They will remind you of how special you are and help you to stay strong and stay the course."

I cried. I felt held by the highest of high. Surely this was the last straw that would bring me out of pain and move me forward. But it didn't.

Now it got serious. I had months of pain with bits of relief, but nothing long-lasting. That's when I heard myself say that I didn't know what was going on. I was brought to my knees, and I finally knew what had to be done. I had to feel the loss of my son. Oh, how I didn't want to go there. But I did.

I was stuck on third base when I dropped into deep lover-land. I was a mess. I felt broken. I would move a bit forward in my healing and then backslide. I was in the grips of a painful dynamic, and it wasn't going away. Then I knew where I was headed—to a very different Shadow Work piece we call a tombstone.

When we love someone and lose them—whether to death or they turned away from us in some way—we hurt. We feel the loss of connection. When we feel this painful separation, we want to find some way—any way—to stay connected.

Because we love them so much and don't ever want to lose the connection with them, we take on a way to never let them go. This can look like addictions, behaviors our loved ones displayed, or sickness they possessed.

With this scenario, my son didn't have hip pain, but this limitation I was feeling kept me from moving on and from creating a new life. In some crazy way, I thought if I fully moved on (subconsciously, that is), I was letting go of my son. I finally figured it out. That's what had me in this never-ending loop.

How Could I Go On and Be Happy After I Lost My Son?

The tombstone is a powerful process that allows us to change how we stay connected to the ones we've loved and lost. I knew that I could find a different way of honoring our relationship and live life again, so I dove into this powerful healing piece.

My son was the main part now. I went to him and spoke to him (figuratively) about holding onto this pattern as a way to never lose him. I told him I loved him and didn't want to let him go. I asked for forgiveness for anything I did that made him leave me.

Suffice it to say, I was weeping big-time. Then I heard him say to me, "Let it go. It isn't going to help our relationship if you stay stuck. Go on with your life. Do what I'm doing, and do what you want." Ah, the new way to stay connected. If I do what he is doing, I can feel him and love him. I don't have to mourn him. I can actually live fully as a way to connect with him.

I then pulled this nagging hip pain metaphorically out of my body once and for all and took on this new way of being with him. I heard myself say, "I choose to move forward, and that has nothing to do with losing my son." Once again, I felt strong, whole, and ready to step more strongly into my life.

We say in Shadow Work that if we can love painfully, we can choose to love in any way we want. We will love because love is who we are. Just because I move forward with my life doesn't mean I'm not loving my son.

I wish I could tell you I am on home base. I am close. My hip pain is gone, but there is still a thread holding me back now located in the center of my lower spine. I may not know what it is yet, but I deeply trust it will be revealed when I am fully ready to let go of whatever it is that remains.

I will say that since I did the tombstone, I have days of no pain at all. I'm back at the gym, I'm focused, and obviously, I have written this book.

Pain is our teacher. We just need to listen and show up for the lesson.

-18-

You're Not Spiritual if You're Angry!

"When you judge another, you do not define them, you define yourself."
— Wayne Dyer

Something is happening with people devoted to their spiritual path that's not cool and that is, frankly, dangerous: a lot of "spiritual" people are running around judging others that embrace their emotions. (I could write a whole book on this topic!)

If they see someone expressing their anger or sadness or any emotion other than joy, their opinion seems to be that they are not divinely connected. If it isn't positive, it must be bad.

People are Putting Their Humanity into Shadow

I think this is a YES/AND issue. Yes, if you are acting out in some unhealthy way, you have forgotten the truth of who you really are, and you are not "being spiritual." If you know you are part of the Divine and are conscious, you will come from a very different place of expression. We are one. You are them and they are you. Period.

Here is the "and" part: you can be spiritual AND feel anger, sadness, fear, shame, and joy!

When you're aware, you can access your healthy Warrior to take a stand and set boundaries, and there is nothing less spiritual about that! If you are conscious, you can even share your judgments using Clean Talk. Just because you feel something other than peace doesn't mean you fall from grace.

I want to reinforce that there is nothing bad in you at all. Every emotion is a gift and a guide. Embracing all of who you are in a conscious, loving way creates peace. I believe when you wake up and love all your parts, you connect more deeply with the Divine. It's when you push away those "bad" emotions that they slip out and harm others.

I have seen plenty of hippy-dippy, spiritual, earthy, crunchy people totally rage or judge or freak when poked. That doesn't mean they're not good people. It doesn't mean they are not spiritual and loving. They're divine just like you. They are just being human too!

If they learned certain feelings are bad and pushed them away, look out. Those locked-away emotions will be hiding in the shadow bag just waiting to jump out. As I have shared throughout the book, energy will be expressed.

My hope is we will begin to heal our shadows and see each other for the divine creatures we all are. When we slip, let us see there is more healing to be had. May we see in each other the beauty that lies within and have compassion for those that can't see the truth of who they are … yet.

Part Three

"If someone comes along and shoots an arrow into your heart, it's fruitless to stand there and yell at the person. It would be much better to turn your attention to the fact that there's an arrow in your heart."
— Pema Chödrön

-19-

Waking Up

"Each aspect within us needs understanding and compassion. If we are unwilling to give it to ourselves how can we expect the world to give it to us? As we are, so is the universe."
– Debbie Ford

It takes courage to open your eyes and question who you really are. Not peeking into the corners of your mind keeps you in the dark and at the mercy of your shadows. It can sting a bit when you look back at your life and see the cost of your choices, but what's at risk if you don't?

Do you want to continue to be led by unhealthy energy? Is it worth experiencing some discomfort in the name of becoming more fully realized? Freedom lies beyond your comfort zone, and your comfort zone isn't so comfy, is it?

You were misled. You were "should" on and didn't know any better. You did the best you could with what you did know back then. The good news is you now know you were fed false information and can choose differently today. Tomorrow isn't here, and today is the beginning of a whole new chapter for you.

Exercise:
How to keep you on your
transformational path

Grab your journal.

It's time to reflect.

Like in the book A Christmas Carol, imagine it's Christmas Day and the future hasn't happened.

Look to the past and make a list of the nasty thoughts you've had about yourself. What has your inner critic told you through the years that hurt you? What were some of the critical messages you told yourself that sucked the joy from your heart and kept you from standing in your power?

Now, look back to see the missed opportunities, the pain, and the price you paid for not knowing the truth of who you are. Look at the cost of believing you weren't good enough or that you were bad in some way.

Now to the future...

Can you imagine what your life will be like if you continue to feed yourself lies about you not being good enough?
What does a future like that hold for you?

Will it keep you from finding a new love because you think you're too old or unworthy?

What poor choices or thoughts from the past, brought into the future, will cost you even more if you continue like that?

Is that what you want?

Of course not. Now, take a breath and see that it's today, not yesterday, and you have options for tomorrow. You can be grateful that today is the beginning of the rest of your life and begin to rewire the old messages right now.

This reflective Magician exercise helps to keep you awake. You don't want to go back to sleep. Taking this time to become aware of the price you've paid in the past can help you choose differently as you take your next steps into your future.

Seeing the journey through your Magician's eyes will create a desire to stay on your healing path and continue to let go of all the old stories that no longer serve you.

The Matrix

Remember the moment in The Matrix movie when Neo, the main character, was given a choice between two pills? If he chose the blue pill, he would stay asleep to the truth. If he swallowed the red pill, he would uncover a whole new universe. He would see with new eyes.

By reading this book, you swallowed the red pill. Welcome to Wonderland.

Just like Neo, you chose to wake up and put on new lenses to see your life differently. Congratulations. It takes courage to stay awake. Going back to sleep isn't a choice anymore. You know too much. You know the price of closing your eyes. There's no going back—and why would you want to?

You finally know you've been programmed and you can undo it. How cool! You can live fully, joyously, and consciously!

By building a stronger relationship with your Sovereign Self, you can feel your worthiness more and more and embrace the preciousness of your life. If someone says boo to you, you can see it as the silly illusion it is and let it go.

By strengthening your relationship with your Warrior, you can access your inner power, which protects you. You set healthy boundaries, granting yourself the ability to successfully move toward your dreams.

By connecting more and more to your vulnerable self, you open your heart and receive the blessings life has to offer you, and if you need help, you can relax in the arms of your Sovereign. You can reach out for your Warrior and have your Magician and Risk Manager guide you.

By dancing with your fear, you see more clearly. If you see risks, do a risk analysis with your Risk Manager.

Your whole posse is available and thrilled to be serving you!

You Can Love Your Whole Package

All your parts are welcome, necessary, and deeply valued. When awake, you can access all of yourself and live consciously and freely.

I missed out on a lot because of my fear of being inadequate. When you begin to look at your life, you too might feel something about the cost of your programming. You might feel sad about what you missed out on. You might feel angry. You might feel fear that it can happen again. You also might feel joy that healing is possible and new things are coming your way.

Whatever you feel, by now you know it's OK to feel your feelings. Embrace them and allow yourself to be in your truth. Let the doors swing open to your healthy board members. Let them lead you consciously on the pathway to a freely expressed life. Let them support your soul to fly free.

My hope is you have compassion for why you made those choices to begin with. You did what was best for you. You wanted to be loved and feel safe. You took great care of yourself the best you knew how, and now you know that some of the old strategies that got you to this point are obsolete and that there is a price to the old wiring. That's great news.

There are layers to healing. Each layer that's exposed and transformed leads you to a more fully realized life. Just when you think you've gotten to the true source of your wound, there could be another layer to unpeel. It's all good!

I have been on this healing path for years. I am thrilled with where I am today and sometimes shocked at how far I have come. The first step was realizing I needed help and finding the courage to get it.

-20-

A Risk Worth Taking

"Don't ask yourself what the world needs,
ask yourself what makes you come alive. And
then go and do that. Because what the world
needs is people who have come alive."
– Howard Washington Thurman

I saw I was living a half-life filled with anxiety. I got to the point where the cost was too high, and I said, "Enough is enough!" Once I hit rock bottom and saw the consequences to my marriage, my kid, my career, and everything else that mattered to me, the universe showed me the way. For me, the path led to Shadow Work, and the doors to heaven on earth opened.

There's risk in looking under the covers and seeing why you are the way you are. It can hurt when you finally see the wiring and the cost. It takes courage to question your beliefs.

The question is, is it worth the risk? If you don't look under the covers and learn how to tame your monster, what will happen to you? As you know, by looking the other way, your monster remains ready to pop out.

What's Next for You?

I truly hope it's the beginning of a new life chapter for you. If there is one message that I hope has sunk in as you read this book, it is healing is possible, and your journey has been a blessing.

It's too damn easy to beat ourselves up for the missed opportunities. Yes, you've made choices through the years, and perhaps a great cost has been associated with those decisions, but your path has brought you here today. Those strategies you used to help you fit in, be loved, and be safe got you here, and now you have new choices! You get to create your life from a more conscious, empowered place.

You had the courage to look at your monster under the covers and now know how to disarm it!

You had the willingness to admit something is not working in your life and picked up this book!

You now know you are not broken!

As I write this last chapter, I'm filled with such joy, and the tears are flowing. I had my doubts about my ability to write this book. I bumped up against my own insecurities. My "not good enough" monster poked me many times along the way, but I kept dancing with it. I knew this book had to be written.

Who am I to write this book? Who am I not to?

It was important for me to write with hopes that I would inspire and impact you at a deep level. I want you to have options and to know that the old programming is bullshit. You can have a wonderful life filled with massive fulfillment … once you learn to tame your inner demons. I wish you a most magical new life chapter filled with transformation and love.

ABOUT THE AUTHOR

Junie Moon has been called the Inner Critic Tamer and Self-Love Expert. She helps people create a life that is passionate, authentic, and fulfilling by teaching them how to turn down the volume on their inner critic, which allows them the freedom to do whatever they dream possible and to feel more love.

She is a transformational coach, Certified Shadow Work® Facilitator, speaker, published co-author of the Amazon #1 best-selling book *Journey to Joy*, creator of the Mission IS-Possible coaching program, and producer/writer of the short film *Shed the Shame* released in 2016.

She is a graduate of the Robbins/Madanes Institute for Strategic Intervention and received her Shadow Work training from Shadow Work® Seminars.

Junie received her BA in psychology from the University of Denver and is a graduate of The New York College of Acupuncture, becoming a licensed massage therapist. Junie continued her education, receiving her master's of science from Tri-State College of Acupuncture. She is also an ordained interfaith minister and a mom.

For over twenty-five years, Junie has been in service to others in their healing and empowerment. She has been on the faculty of numerous women's empowerment events and continues to create sacred places for people to grow and heal. Junie also lectures at corporations throughout the tri-state area on the tools for creating a fulfilling life.

Junie Moon works with clients one-on-one in her private coaching practice both virtually and in person. She also offers workshops and retreats and speaks throughout the country.

It is her passion to help others realize their truest potential and create the life they so deeply desire. Junie Moon absolutely adores seeing people embrace life fully, bringing them better jobs, healthier relationships, and massive joy. Her clients step powerfully into their soul purpose with grace and ease, which delights her to the core.

Loving the
Whole Package

4 Week Online Course

Learn how to:

- Quiet your Inner Critic
- Trust your gut
- Feel your feelings
- Know your truth
- Allow love to flow in
- Honor your journey
- Embrace all your parts-inside and out

Junie Moon Schreiber
Inner Critic Tamer
Contact: junie@midlifeloveoutloud.com

Online Course

CONNECT WITH THE AUTHOR

I'm thrilled when people reach out for support and want to know more about this work. Being on a healing path takes courage and commitment, so I want you to know you don't have to do it alone. I'm here to help you stay on track. I encourage you to reach out. Let me know how you're doing, and tell me how I can be of service. I look forward to being part of your journey. We are not meant to do it alone.

Email: Junie@midlifeloveoutloud.com

Business Phone: (973) 464-8739

Social Media:
Facebook: www.facebook.com/midlifeloveoutloud
LinkedIn: https://www.linkedin.com/in/love-coach-junie-moon-995262a/
Twitter: @CoachJunieMoon
Instagram: midlifeloveoutloud
YouTube: https://www.youtube.com/@MidlifeLoveOutLoud

ACKNOWLEDGEMENTS

It's funny that writing this part of the book is the hardest of all. I don't want to miss a soul.

This is my first book, and it was quite the adventure to get to this point! Without the support of my friends and family, as well as all my wonderful life teachers who helped me know my worthiness along the way, this could not have happened. With that said, there are a few people I must highlight.

I really want to thank Cliff Barry for teaching me the Shadow Work® model and blessing me with this amazing opportunity of writing this book to share its principles. You're a phenomenal mentor, but more importantly, you're also a friend. I also want to acknowledge Vicki Woodard, his righthand woman, who also trained me through the years. Both of you created a safe, loving environment for me to learn this powerful work and to grow as a human being. I'm forever grateful.

I want to acknowledge Todd Lewis for holding my hand through this writing journey. When I hit my walls of fear and self-doubt, you brought me back to my center and reminded me I could do it. Your love, support, and insights were priceless.

I also want acknowledge Karin Green, a fellow shadow worker, for helping me fine-tune some of the Shadow Work® principles in my editing phase. You were a great help. Thank you for your keen eye and your friendship.

A huge thanks to all my friends and family who continually love me and keep me on my life path. Without you, this book could not be written. Your love and support fills my heart and my cup runneth over.

I also want to acknowledge the two women who have influenced my life in ways words cannot begin to describe: ALisa Starkweather for your love and the introduction to this work, and MeriLynn Blum, for being my life guide. I truly would not be where I am today without you both.

Lastly, to my "wasband," Louis Conselatore. Thank you for allowing me to include you in this book. My life story is not complete without you. Your support continues to blow my mind, and I am grateful for every moment we have shared on this planet. May there be many more ...

REFERENCES

Ball, Lucille "Love yourself first and everything else falls into line. You really have to love yourself to get anything done in this world." www.positivityblog.com

Bloom, Amy "You are imperfect. Permanently and inevitably flawed. And you are beautiful." www.Google.com

Braiker, Henry B. "Conflict avoidance is not the hallmark of a good relationship. On the contrary, it is a symptom of serious problems and poor communication." www.Google.com

Brown, Brene "Courage starts with showing up and letting ourselves be seen." www.Google.com

"Healing is not an overnight process, it is a daily cleansing of pain, it is a daily healing of your life." www.azquotes.com

Buddha "We are shaped by our thoughts; we become what we think. When the mind is pure, joy follows like a shadow that never leaves." www.brainyquote.com

Butcher, Jim "Anger is just anger. It isn't good. It isn't bad. It just is. What you do with it is what matters." www.Google.com

Chödrön, Pema "If someone comes along and shoots an arrow into your heart, it's fruitless to stand there and yell at the person. It would be much better to turn your attention to the fact that there's an arrow in your heart."

Start Where You Are: A Guide to Compassionate Living
www.goodreads.com

Dispenza, Joe "By Itself, Conscious Positive Thinking Cannot Overcome Subconscious Negative Feelings."
Breaking the Habit of Being Yourself: How to Lose Your Mind and Create a New One
www.Goodreads.com

Dyer, Wayne There's nothing wrong with anger provided you use it constructively." www.addicted2success.com
"When you judge another, you do not define them, you define yourself."
www.awakening-intuiton.com

Ford, Debbie "As you continue the work of acknowledging and claiming the gifts of your past and standing in the power of your present, you are freeing up enormous reserves of creative energy."
www.good reads.com
"When divine consciousness enters, the shift occurs and you will be engulfed by what will feel like the greatest love imaginable – a love in which your soul realigns with your spirit and they meet together as one."
www.goodreads.com
"Our society nurtures the illusion that all the rewards go to the people who are perfect. But many of us are finding out that trying to be perfect is costly."
www.goodreads.com
"You must go into the dark in order to bring forth your light."
www.goodreads.com
"Whatever we refuse to recognize about ourselves has a way of rearing its head and making itself known when we least expect it."
www.goodreads.com
"Each aspect within us needs understanding and compassion. If we are unwilling to give it to ourselves how can we expect the world to give it to us? As we are, so is the universe." www.Feminine1st.com

Gawain, Shakti "When I'm trusting and being myself as fully as possible, everything in my life reflects this by falling into place easily, often miraculously."
www.brainyquotes.com

Hay, Louise L. "You have been criticizing yourself for years, and it hasn't worked. Try approving of yourself and see what happens."
www.good reads.com

Jobs, Steve "Great things in business are never done by one person. They're done by a team of people."
www.brainyquote.com

Jung, C.G. "One does not become enlightened by imagining figures of light, but by making the darkness conscious. The latter procedure, however, is disagreeable and therefore not popular."
www.goodreads.com
"Everything that irritates us about others can lead us to understanding ourselves." www.brainyquote.com

Kagan, Anne "A shift in perspective makes the particles in your universe dance to new possibilities."
The Afterlife of Billy Fingers
www.Google.com

Keen, Sam "What happens if I try to build a life dedicated to avoiding all danger and all unnecessary risk?"
www.Picturequotes.com

Laughton, Geoff "Avoiding conflict to try to "keep the peace" is a surefire way to gradually destroy your relationship."
Building a Conflict-Proof Relationship

Lincoln, Abraham "Character is like a tree and reputation like a shadow. The shadow is what we think of it; the tree is the real thing."
www.addicted2success.com

Lipton, Dr. Bruce "The moment you change your perception, is the moment you rewrite the chemistry of your body."
www.manifestintuition.com

Lama, Dalai "Great love and great achievements involve great risks."
ww.verybestquotes.com

McGill, Bryant "Real transformation requires real honesty. If you want to move forward, get real with yourself."
www.Google.com

www.merriam-webster.com
"A sharp and often satirical utterance designed to cut or give pain."

Nin, Anaïs "And the day came when the risk to remain tight in a bud was more painful than the risk it took to blossom."
www.Google.com

Parton, Dolly "Being a star just means that you just find your own special place, and that you shine where you are. To me, that's what being a star means."
www.brainyquotes.com

Pinkola Estés, Clarissa "We find that by opening the door to the shadow realm a little, and letting out various elements a few at a time, relating to them, finding use for them, negotiating, we can reduce being surprised by shadow sneak attacks and unexpected explosions."
Women Who Run With the Wolves: Myths and Stories of the Wild Woman Archetype
www.good reads.com

Robbins, Tony "It is in your moments of decision that your destiny is shaped."
www.addicted2success.com
"Where focus goes, energy flows."
www.addicted2success.com

"Let fear be a counselor, not a jailer."
www.addicted2success.com
"Your past does not equal your future."
www.addicted2success.com
"It's not the events of our lives that shape us, but our beliefs as to what those events mean."
www.brainyquote.com

Roth, Kagan, Anne "A shift in perspective makes the particles in your universe dance to new possibilities."
The Afterlife of Billy Fingers
www.Google.com

Roth, Geneen "We don't want to EAT hot fudge sundaes as much as we want our lives to BE hot fudge sundaes. We want to come home to ourselves."
Women, Food and God: An Unexpected Path to Almost Everything
www.Goodreads.com

Roth, Geneen "Most of us spend our lives protecting ourselves from losses that have already happened."
www.Goodreads.com

Sarno, Dr. John "There's nothing like a little physical pain to keep your mind off your emotional problems."
www.Goodreads.com

www.shadowwork.com
"The term 'shadow' was first used by Carl G. Jung to describe the repressed or denied part of the Self. Robert Bly popularized this idea in A Little Book on the Human Shadow. According to Bly, it was as if we threw these unacceptable qualities over our shoulder into a bag, which we've been dragging around behind us ever since."

Unknown "Teamwork makes the dream work."
www.Picturequotes.com

Von Ebner-Eschenbach, Marie "Pain is a great teacher of mankind. Beneath its breath, souls develop."
www.azquotes.com

Washington Thurman, Howard "Don't ask yourself what the world needs, ask yourself what makes you come alive. And then go and do that. Because what the world needs is people who have come alive."
www.beliefnet.com/quotes

Williamson, Marianne "Our deepest fear is not that we are inadequate. Our deepest fear is that we are powerful beyond measure. It is our light, not our darkness that most frightens us. We ask ourselves, 'Who am I to be brilliant, gorgeous, talented, fabulous?'"
www.Goodreads.com

Wolfgang von Goethe, Johann, **Götz von Berlichingen** "There is strong shadow where there is much light."
www.good reads.com

Wyland "The ocean stirs the heart, inspires the imagination and brings eternal joy to the soul."
www.Google.com

Support and Other Resources

We are not meant to walk this journey alone. We need each other. This book is one resource, and the toolbox is there for you to dive deeper into these practices.

I encourage you to get one-on-one coaching. When you have someone in your court to guide you—an outside Magician, if you will—it's powerful. We can only see what we can see. Those shadows are slippery and sneaky, and they love to hide. Having a skilled shadow worker to look objectively at your patterns can speed up your transformation in a big way!

Having some individual support can have a monumental effect on your personal development. Get it. You're worth it, and I would love to be by your side to help you transform those shadows.

If you want to discuss a deeper coaching relationship, go to www.midlifeloveoutloud.com and we can have a conversation about your next steps.

Stay active in the Facebook group too. It keeps you on your toes and helps you remain awake to what's possible. Also, having a tribe of other courageous souls on the path of self-discovery and personal transformation is extremely supportive.

Check out www.ShadowWork.com. It has a ton of additional resources. You can read great articles, grab the *Clean Talk* CD, learn about Shadow Work trainings, and so much more.